INCREDIBLE DOG JOURNEYS

Laura Greaves is a multi-award winning journalist, author and proud 'crazy dog lady'. She has spent nearly twenty years writing for newspapers and magazines in Australia and around the world and is the former editor of *Dogs Life* magazine. A freelance writer for the past seven years, Laura has written extensively for countless dog and pet-specific print and web publications. She is also the author of two romantic comedy novels, *Be My Baby* and *The Ex-Factor* (published by Penguin Random House's Destiny Romance imprint), both of which feature an extensive supporting cast of cheeky canines.

Find out more at www.lauragreaves.com
and www.facebook.com/lauragreaveswritesbooks

LAURA GREAVES

INCREDIBLE DOG JOURNEYS

AMAZING TRUE STORIES OF EXCEPTIONAL DOGS

MICHAEL JOSEPH
an imprint of
PENGUIN BOOKS

MICHAEL JOSEPH

UK | USA | Canada | Ireland | Australia
India | New Zealand | South Africa | China

Penguin Books is part of the Penguin Random House group of companies
whose addresses can be found at global.penguinrandomhouse.com.

Penguin
Random House
Australia

First published by Penguin Random House Australia Pty Ltd, 2016

10 9 8 7 6 5 4 3 2 1

Text copyright © Laura Greaves, 2016

Cover design by Louisa Maggio © Penguin Random House Australia Pty Ltd
Text design by Samantha Jayaweera © Penguin Random House Australia Pty Ltd
Cover photographs: landscape by Janelle Lugge/shutterstock; dog on front cover by
Eriklam/iStock; dog on back cover by Joanne Lefson, www.oscarsarc.org
Typeset in Sabon by Jouve India
Colour separation by Splitting Image Colour Studio, Clayton, Victoria
Printed and bound in Australia by Griffin Press, an accredited ISO AS/NZS 14001
Environmental Management Systems printer.

National Library of Australia
Cataloguing-in-Publication data:

Greaves, Laura, author
Incredible dog journeys / Laura Greaves
9780143797258 (paperback)
Dogs – Behaviour
Dogs – Anecdotes
Human-animal relationships – Anecdotes
Pet loss

636.7

penguin.com.au

*For those of us striving to be the kind
of people our dogs think we are*

CONTENTS

INTRODUCTION

My first love was a boy called Freddie. He was handsome, cheeky and more than a little mischievous. Freddie had confidence. He had swagger.

Ours was a long-distance relationship. Freddie lived on a farm near Naracoorte, in the south-east corner of South Australia. I lived in Adelaide, 'the big smoke'. But I loved him fiercely from afar.

Then, as is inevitable in great love stories, tragedy struck. There was a terrible accident: Freddie fell from a speeding ute and suffered horrific injuries. One of his legs was shattered. He would likely never walk again, if he survived at all.

Freddie's family gathered to consider their options. Finally, they reached an agonising consensus: Freddie would have to be put down.

Did I mention Freddie was a sheepdog?

He was a kelpie, and the hardest working dog on my relatives' vast property. Freddie worked tirelessly from dawn until dusk, and he would have worked all night too if given the chance.

When news of Freddie's imminent demise reached me, I was distraught. So I did what any writer would do, and penned him a farewell letter. *Dear Freddie*, it began, *get well soon. I love you.*

Did I mention I was five?

I sent my letter to Freddie and waited, hoping against hope for a miracle that would save my beloved.

Weeks passed. Finally, a letter arrived from Naracoorte. *Dear Laura*, it said, *thank you for your letter. I am feeling much better and will be back on the ute in no time*. It was signed with a paw print.

It seemed like divine intervention. In reality, Freddie's survival was down to an excellent veterinarian who had amputated the dog's ruined leg and put the rest of him back together with steel rods and pins. He really was back on the ute in no time, and he was still the best dog on the farm, even on three legs.

I was much older when I really grasped the significance of this. Farmers love their working dogs, but they are workers first and foremost. If they can't do the job, there's no place for them.

But something in my letter to Freddie had touched his owner, a middle-aged career farmer who, while always kind, was pragmatic above all else. Though I adored Freddie, he was in many ways unremarkable, and he'd already had a good innings. My cousin could have had Freddie put to sleep – should have, some might argue – but he didn't.

Instead, he spent thousands of dollars saving a broken dog, simply because that dog meant something to a little girl. My juvenile passion for dogs meant Freddie's life – his journey – was able to continue for many more years. As I grew up and came to understand that, in my way, I had saved Freddie, it was a powerful lesson not only in the myriad ways dogs enrich our lives, but also in our responsibility to them.

As the stories in this collection illustrate, dogs will do anything for their humans, and their canine friends, and they ask for so little in return.

Dogs' journeys take many different forms. They may strive for months or even years to return to beloved owners. They may overcome seemingly insurmountable obstacles to save themselves or others. Or they may live quiet lives on farms or in suburban backyards.

The tracing of every incredible dog journey involves a certain amount of detective work. In many cases, all that is definitely known is that a dog disappeared in one place and turned up in another. What actually happened in the intervening days, months or even years is really anybody's guess. And until our canine counterparts learn to speak, that will have to do.

Of course, there are often clues. Sometimes a missing canine will be spotted in the throes of his odyssey – a fleeting glimpse of a dog on a mission whose objective is known only to him. Or there might be physical markers of the places he's been and the things he's seen: injuries, dirt and debris that hint at what he went through to get home to his people.

And then there is the dog himself. Big or small, young or old, pedigree or 'bitser', one thing all dogs have in spades is character. It's that character that can be most useful in helping to piece together what an incredible dog journey may have entailed. After all, as American president Dwight D. Eisenhower once said, 'What counts is not necessarily the size of the dog in the fight; it's the size of the fight in the dog.'

Wherever they are, whatever they do, a dog's journey is always extraordinary, because dogs have a capacity to love, and to be loved, that is unlike any other animal.

Sharing a dog's incredible journey, in whatever form it takes, is an enormous privilege. I truly hope I never have to spend a day without at least one dog by my side. Dogs want nothing more than to be our companions on our respective journeys. Returning that favour is the least we can do.

Laura Greaves, 2016

RIDIN' THE RAILS

OCCY'S STORY

It was, as they say in the classics, a dark and stormy night. As she drove north on the M1 Pacific Motorway in early November after a job interview in Sydney, teacher Belinda 'Binny' Murray was starting to worry. Ahead of her, leaden clouds the colour of charcoal menaced the horizon. They were thunderheads, no doubt about it. And they were scudding across the sky toward Binny's hometown, Newcastle – and toward Occy, the acutely astraphobic dog in her care there.

Occy belonged to Binny's close friend Philippa Johnston and her husband, Nathan. With Philippa and her baby daughter, Audrey, on holiday in New Zealand, and Nathan on deployment to the Middle East with the Royal Australian Air Force, Binny was on dogsitting duty. She was right to feel uneasy that afternoon: she had looked after Occy on a number of occasions and knew that the two-year-old Staffordshire bull terrier cross was petrified of thunderstorms.

The start of October marks the arrival of storm season in New South Wales. Right through the summer months, dramatic electrical storms are a weekly or even daily occurrence from south of the ACT, through Sydney and right up to the Queensland border. Every year, on average, severe thunderstorms cause more than $100 million worth of damage in NSW and the ACT. The Hunter region, with Newcastle smack dab in the middle, is the most storm-affected area in the state.

By the time they had departed for a friend's wedding in New Zealand in early November 2014, summer's streak of spectacular tempests was already becoming run of the mill for Philippa and baby Audrey. Occy, however, wasn't quite so blasé about the thick black clouds that gathered every afternoon, nor the booming thunder and incandescent lightning that came with them.

Just a couple of weeks before, Occy had escaped the large, fenced yard of the family's Georgetown home during a storm. On that occasion he was lucky: Philippa was at home and quickly managed to find him. But the storms were relentless that summer, and Occy had tried to flee the terror in the sky again and again during the ten days Binny had been staying with him. He had access to an enclosed, dry garage when nobody was home, but as far as poor Occy was concerned, making a break for it was his only option.

Not wanting to take any chances, Binny and the Johnstons' neighbours had rigged up a makeshift fortress around the front gate – which seemed to be Occy's most likely escape route – raising the height of the fence to over six feet. Now, as the heavens opened and sheeting rain swept across the freeway, Binny's sense of unease grew. All she could do was hope her temporary barrier held out.

As she ploughed on towards Newcastle in what felt like slow motion, Binny punched a friend's number into her phone. 'I was panicked, so I called my friend and begged her to go and see if Occy was still at Philippa's house,' she says. 'Unfortunately she couldn't get there, but she assured me he would be okay. I wasn't convinced, and I couldn't stop thinking about him. The thunderstorm was so intense and I just had a bad feeling he wouldn't be there when I got home.'

At last, Binny drove into the narrow street lined with pretty weatherboard cottages where Philippa and Nathan lived. She felt a flicker of hope as she saw that the fortifications over the front gate were still in place.

Shouting Occy's name over the crashing thunder and torrential rain, Binny raced into the garden. She ran a lap of the house, searching all of Occy's usual hiding spots. But he wasn't there. Somehow, the Houdini-like hound had breached the reinforced perimeter.

Occy was out there, alone, in the storm.

For Philippa, animals have been a constant in a life marked by adventure and upheaval. Growing up, her father worked for international machinery corporation Caterpillar and his job took the family all over the world. Born in New Zealand, Philippa spent her formative years in Indonesia, Thailand and the United States. With every new location came a new school and a new set of friends, but one friend who never left her side was the family's Shetland sheepdog, Titan.

'Titan was one when we got him and he lived to be sixteen. We had a very close relationship – he was literally my best friend. He got hit by a car when he was one and I remember putting my blanket on him to keep him warm. I used to share my ice-creams with him, much to my mum's horror,' Philippa says.

'Every new place we moved to, Titan came with us. We used to joke that when we die we want to come back as an expat's dog or cat, because they have a pretty good life. I'm used to being a travelling gypsy. Animals become your constant – your family.'

Later, she rescued a kitten, Bugsy, who also became a devoted companion. 'He was from a litter of six and the mother didn't take to them, so only two survived. He was the little runt and I fell in love with him.'

For years, it was Philippa and Bugsy against the world. Then she met Nathan – much to the finicky feline's dismay. 'There was definitely a period of adjustment for Bugsy when I met the boyfriend, who then moved in and became the husband,' she laughs.

Nathan originally hails from Norfolk Island, though his career in the RAAF has meant he's used to moving around, too. He's also an animal lover – 'He has this thing about rescue dogs,' says Philippa – and had long been keen to adopt a dog as soon as he and Philippa found themselves in one place long enough to give it some proper thought.

They got their chance in 2011, when Nathan was posted to RAAF Base Williamtown, 15 kilometres north of the coal port city of Newcastle. As famous for its stunning surf beaches and proximity to the world-renowned Hunter Valley wine region as for its coal, Newcastle instantly felt like home to the couple – and Bugsy. After buying their home in the smart suburb of Georgetown, the search for a new four-legged family member began in earnest.

A staffy was at the top of Nathan's wishlist. 'He grew up with dogs and really loves them. He'd had a cattle dog, but had always loved staffies. He's very sporty and was after a "nuggety" dog,' Philippa says.

Surfing fanatic Nathan even had a name picked out: Occy, the nickname of his surfing hero, former world champion Mark Occhilupo.

Philippa first spotted Occy's brother, Mercury, on the Facebook page of Sydney-based rescue group Fetching Dogs. He was in foster care at Strathfield, a suburb in Sydney's inner-west, and she made plans to go and visit him.

'We went down to see Mercury, but of course we fell in love with the cheeky, naughty one instead,' she says. 'Mercury seemed quiet and calm, while Occy was the really active one. They were both very affectionate and had a great relationship with each other. It was really hard not to walk out of there with both of them, but we didn't think we had enough space at the time.'

There was also Bugsy to consider. By now a statesman-like twelve year old, he'd already faced a huge adjustment when Nathan appeared on the scene. Coping with a dog as well was a big ask, but two dogs? Not going to happen.

And so, in September 2012, three-month-old Occy came home to Newcastle, and Philippa and Nathan were quickly beguiled by his happy-go-lucky approach to life. While his precise breed mix remains a mystery, the staffy in him is obvious – from his infectious grin to the ceaseless wagging of his tail. Philippa suspects there's some Bull Arab or per-haps even labrador in there, too. Occy certainly has a lab's laidback approach to life – except where thunderstorms are concerned. That sensitive soul is pure staffy.

Occy may be goofy, but he's also smart. He knows who's the disciplinarian of the household and who's the clown. 'He's my dog in terms of being a good boy – he listens to me the most with "come, sit, stay" – but when it comes to play-ing he's all about Nathan,' says Philippa.

'He gets really spoilt. It's like, "Mum feeds me and washes me, but Dad's where the fun is." He's mostly an out-side dog, but we do terrible things like letting him in our room at night.'

Even Bugsy warmed to his new canine sibling, sleeping on top of Occy's crate whenever the newcomer was inside it. 'Bugsy was the grandpa of the family; he was a bit of a boss, but they developed a really good friendship. They spent most of their days lying about half a metre a part. They pretended they didn't like each other, but really they did.'

Bugsy's quick acceptance of Occy was an added relief when, just two months after the puppy joined the family, Philippa discovered she was pregnant. Watching her choosy cat welcome Occy to the fold made her certain both animals would cope well with the imminent arrival of their human 'sister'.

Audrey was born in late 2013, and Occy was instantly smitten. 'They have a really lovely bond. He's very patient with her,' says Philippa.

In 2014, Nathan left home for seven months on deployment. It was a stressful time for the family, with Audrey not yet one and Philippa returning to part-time work. Somehow, Occy seemed to understand. 'He definitely felt it. He knew he was missing a part of his family.'

After Nathan's departure, Occy developed a sudden aversion to the summer thunderstorms that rattled the skies over Newcastle most days. And when Philippa and Audrey went to New Zealand in November, Occy grew even more anxious.

'He never used to be afraid of thunderstorms, but I think the stress of Nathan being away started to make him a bit sensitive. Then when Audrey and I were away on top of that it got worse.'

It was perhaps a perfect storm of anxiety and loneliness. The arrival of yet another *real* storm on that Wednesday afternoon was more than Occy could bear.

*

Binny had looked everywhere. The storm that spooked Occy had long passed, but still she traipsed through the streets of Georgetown and its neighbouring suburbs searching for any trace of the terrified dog.

'I spent all afternoon and all night looking for him. I called local vets and pounds several times, and went to the local RSPCA shelters to make sure he wasn't there. I asked neighbours to keep an eye out for him and searched all his usual hiding spots, but there was no sign of him,' she says.

'All that was going through my mind was how I could possibly tell Pip he wasn't at home. I felt so guilty. I was worried that I hadn't done enough to find him, and that I'd let her down. Occy is like a family member, so I knew how upset she would be – and that made *me* more upset. It was probably one of the worst phone calls I have ever had to make.'

But make the call she did, the day after Occy's great escape, reaching Philippa at her mum's house in Christchurch, on New Zealand's South Island. It was Thursday, the night before she and Audrey were due to fly home after their blissful two-week trip. All of a sudden, that return flight couldn't come soon enough for Philippa.

'I felt horrible that Binny had spent two days feeling sad and stressed, trying to find him,' says Philippa. 'I felt so far away and I was just thinking, *Gosh, will I ever see him again?* If you haven't found a missing dog within a couple of hours there's no need to panic just yet, but after two days it starts to get a bit scary.'

Every awful scenario imaginable ran through her mind. Had Occy injured himself on the tall fence in his desperation to get out? Was he hiding somewhere, hurt and afraid? They were just a kilometre from Waratah train station – what if he'd made his way onto the train tracks and . . . just thinking about it was horrifying.

'That's what I worried about – not just that Occy was out there and didn't have anywhere to go, but cars and really scary stuff like theft and dog fighting. Even though he looks like a tough dog, he's not,' she says.

Philippa also faced another dilemma. Just as Binny had delayed calling her, she now wrestled with when – or even *if* – she should call Nathan overseas and tell him his beloved dog was missing. Finally, she decided to hold off on telling him at least until she was at home and could make some decisions about what to do next.

'Nathan is the type of person who wants to fix things, and I knew he would want to be back home with me trying to find Occy. Not being able to do that would have made things even tougher for him over there.'

So, after a sleepless night, Philippa packed her bags and prepared to travel back to Newcastle on Friday morning. Even if all she could do was relieve Binny from her hopeful patrols of the streets of Georgetown, at least she could feel she was doing something to bring Occy home.

Then, just an hour before she was due to leave for the airport, Philippa's phone rang. Her heart leapt into her throat as the caller identified herself as RSPCA Inspector

Claudia Jones. She had found a very scared staffy cross limping along the train tracks in a rail yard with severely injured paws – and Philippa's phone number was on the tag hanging from his collar.

Philippa was ecstatic, but worried about the seriousness of Occy's injuries. 'Claudia said he was a bit hurt, and asked if I'd mind if she took him to the vet. I said that would be great and gave her the details for Occy's regular vet in the next suburb, Hamilton.'

There was a pause at the other end of the line. 'Where?' Claudia asked eventually.

'Hamilton,' Philippa repeated. 'Where are you calling from?' The RSPCA has a shelter at Rutherford, about 30 minutes' drive from Hamilton, and a veterinary hospital at Tighes Hill, just five minutes away by car.

Claudia told Philippa she was in Auburn. 'And I was thinking, *Where in Newcastle is that?*'

Then the penny dropped. Claudia was in Auburn in Sydney – and that meant Occy was, too.

It was surely impossible, but the injuries to Occy's feet seemed to confirm it: the determined dog had run away during a storm in Newcastle on November 5, and he hadn't stopped running until he reached the inner-western suburbs of Sydney, two days later and more than 170 kilometres away.

The trip from Auburn Maintenance Centre to the closest vet hospital was the easiest part of Occy's journey; he got to do that in the air-conditioned comfort of Claudia's RSPCA transport van. If the sorry state of his paws was any indication, however, getting from Newcastle to the enormous depot sandwiched between Auburn and Clyde railway stations, where the Sydney Trains fleet is maintained, had been a vastly more gruelling expedition.

Occy was spotted wandering along the train tracks by workers at the rail yard, but he fled into a large pipe when approached; they couldn't get near him. He was limping, seemed disoriented and was clearly terrified. The workers could see he was wearing a collar, though, and that dangling from that collar was an identification tag. Not wanting to stress or frighten the poor, injured dog any further, they had backed off and called the RSPCA.

Claudia managed to catch Occy, and after her astonishing phone call with Philippa, took him straight to the vet. Occy was severely dehydrated and his paws were terribly blistered, as though he had walked a long distance over very rough or hot terrain. He also had some muscle wastage and was utterly exhausted. This, coupled with the fact that he'd covered such an enormous distance in just two days, certainly seemed to support the hypothesis that he'd run all the way from home.

Though the route along the train line from Newcastle to Sydney is direct, it's far from straightforward. Assuming Occy slipped through the sturdy wire fencing and onto the tracks near Waratah station – the closest passenger platform to his home – he would then have had to make his way through the city's south-western suburbs, crossing the heavily polluted Throsby Creek and its offshoots at least four times and negotiating the enormous Broadmeadow rail yard, dodging trains as he somehow managed to continue following the correct set of Sydney-bound tracks. He would have crossed over or under three major arterial roads before reaching the Newcastle city limits, then traversed another creek and picked his way through one more train depot at Glendale, a suburb at the northern tip of Lake Macquarie.

From Glendale, the line crosses broad Cockle Creek, then skirts the edge of Lake Macquarie itself. As he moved resolutely southward, Occy would surely have been able to smell the salty air above the vast saltwater lagoon to his left; the 110-square-kilometre lake is twice the size of Sydney Harbour. Perhaps he stopped to admire the view. More than likely, he just kept running.

To Occy's right lay . . . not much at all. Vast tracts of impenetrable bushland, the Awaba, Heaton and Olney state forests, and Watagans National Park. And somewhere in the midst of it all, the M1 Pacific Motorway: eight lanes of traffic roaring between Sydney and Brisbane – definitely no place for a dog far from home.

What would Occy have made of the four monolithic turbo-alternators towering over him as he raced by the Eraring Power Station, Australia's largest coal-fired electricity generator? And did he pick up his pace even more a few kilometres later, when the pungent perfume of the Dora Creek Waste-water Treatment Works assailed his sensitive nose?

Occy ploughed on through the Central Coast towns of Morisset and Wyee, chalking up no less than eleven creek crossings before another eye-watering encounter with a sewage treatment plant at Charmhaven.

Who knows whether Occy wandered away from the train tracks to drink from the many waterways on his route? The weather that November was typical of late spring in the subtropical Central Coast region: furnace-hot and outrageously humid during the day, with the sort of violent storms that had sparked Occy's journey in the first place bringing only temporary relief at night. His mouth must have been desert dry, but the extent of his dehydration when he was found indicated he had drunk infrequently or not at all, while the blistering to his paws seemed to suggest he had not only stuck unwaveringly to the train line, but had run directly on the sun-baked steel rails.

Just outside of Wyong, the tracks meet and run parallel to the Pacific Highway, the road that had been the main east-coast transport route before the motorway assumed some of the traffic burden in the 1980s. But cars were the least of Occy's worries here. With their affordable housing and wide-open spaces, the towns of the Central Coast are popular with commuters who travel by train to Sydney every day. During the weekday peak, trains thunder down this part of the line every four minutes. Occy must have made it through by the skin of his teeth.

Could Occy have made part of his journey *onboard* a train? Perhaps he made his way into a carriage, enjoying a brief respite until being chased out by a train guard or disgorged along with the tide of commuters at a Sydney station? It's possible, of course, but it seems unlikely. His physical scars pointed to Occy having made the whole journey under his own steam.

Claudia Jones is also convinced Occy got to Sydney without help. 'Because he was so reluctant to approach strangers it doesn't make sense that he would have hitched a ride, and the muscle fatigue he was showing and the soreness of his feet were consistent with quite a run,' she says.

The track diverges from the Pacific Highway and plunges back into the bush at Tuggerah before picking the road up again at Ourimbah and following it all the way to Gosford. There, the Pacific Highway makes a sharp right turn, wending through the bush before merging with the M1 just past Kariong. The train line, meanwhile, enters the breathtaking Brisbane Water Estuary and hugs the perimeter for almost all of its eighteen stunning kilometres. Passengers' jaws often drop as they take in the spectacular views; Occy was undoubtedly more concerned with making it across the two narrow rail bridges unscathed.

If Occy was spotted at all during his intrepid journey – by a train passenger perhaps, or the driver of a car – no sightings were reported. Then again, the sight of a dog trotting along a train line as locomotives whiz by at 130 km/hr would probably strike most as a figment of the imagination. And if Occy had been seen in this particular location, he would have been a fugitive from justice: this stretch of track bisects the Brisbane Water National Park, and all of Australia's national parks are off-limits to dogs.

After Brisbane Water, Occy crossed the Hawkesbury River via the 890-metre-long, seventy-year-old railway bridge just north of the town of Brooklyn. Then, after a bit more bush bashing and passing over the M1, he finally made it to Sydney's northern outskirts. From there, he hobbled another 40 kilometres or so to Auburn, where his journey mercifully reached its end in Claudia's arms.

Did he pause to sleep on his two-night trek? Did he eat? Was he relieved when he reached Sydney, or simply more confused and frightened than ever? Did he somehow know that Binny, his interim carer, had been there the day he ran away? Just what was he *thinking*?

That Occy was picked up in Auburn, less than 10 kilometres from his former foster home in Strathfield – the last place he saw his brother, Mercury – was not lost on Philippa. Had he fled the storm in Newcastle and, missing his forever family, tried to find the only other family he'd ever known?

'Our best guess is that he followed the tracks all the way. Whether he knew that was where he came from and was trying to get back there, who knows?' she says. 'I think at first it must have been, *I've got to get out of here and get away from this storm* and then, *I don't know where I am so I'd better just keep going this way*. I felt bad because it definitely seemed that he'd been looking for Nathan and me. Only Occy knows for sure.'

*

The drive from Newcastle to Sydney to be reunited with Occy on Saturday was a rollercoaster of emotions for Philippa. She and Audrey had landed in Sydney the night before, but couldn't bring Occy home to Newcastle with them because the vet wanted to keep him overnight for observation. So the next day, she rose at 4 a.m. to go and collect her wandering dog. The trip that had taken Occy two days would take her a little over 90 minutes.

'It was like this crazy Canonball Run. I didn't know whether I was incredibly happy or about to cry again from the whole thing. Probably both – I didn't know what I was doing. I had moments of laughing because I was so happy, and then half an hour later I'd be bawling again,' she says.

Guilt was also gnawing at her; she had decided not to tell Nathan about Occy's ordeal until she had him safely at home. When she had called Nathan the night before to tell him she was safely home from New Zealand, he had asked after Occy. Philippa told him that Occy was 'okay'. Though she knew in her heart the dog found in Auburn was Occy, there was a voice in her head whispering, *What if it's not him?* And she knew it couldn't be silenced until she saw him.

When she finally did, the emotion that washed over her was pure relief – and Occy seemed to feel the same way. He was filthy and fatigued, but his joy was palpable.

'He was so tired, limping, just lying down and resting as much as possible. But his tail was going and he was just so excited to see me, like "Oh gosh, I've found you – or you've found me!"' says Philippa. 'He was just super relieved. You could see that look in his eyes: *I can go home now.*'

Occy and Philippa weren't the only ones who felt an enormous weight had been lifted: Binny was overjoyed that her wayward charge had been located. 'It was absolute joy, excitement and relief, followed by amazement and shock over how he had made his way to Sydney,' she says.

'I still have the same feeling today. I would love to know how he got there. If only he could tell us all.'

With Occy safely back home in Newcastle, Philippa also came clean to Nathan. 'I had to wait until the afternoon to call him and I said, "You know how I told you Occy was okay? Well, he *was* okay – he just wasn't with us." I maintain that wasn't a lie, because I knew he was okay,' she laughs.

In his own unique way, even Bugsy the cat let Occy know he'd been missed. 'Bugsy had his usual attitude,' says Philippa of her long-time feline friend, who sadly passed away in early 2016. 'It was like, "Oh Occy, you're back, are you?" But he definitely hung around Occy for a few days as if to say, "I'm glad you're back, you idiot."'

Occy's paws took several weeks to heal after his ordeal, and his phobia of storms lingered. It wasn't until Nathan returned from deployment a few months later that the dog finally began to relax.

'You could almost hear Occy's sigh of relief when Nathan came home. It was like for all that time he'd been thinking, *I've got to do more to protect the girls while the big man is away*,' she says. 'When he had his number one playmate back, he went back to being his relaxed, happy self. The storm phobia has gotten better, and we're hopeful he may grow out of it.'

Philippa and Nathan welcomed a second daughter, Abigale, in late 2015, and Occy has become just as attached to her as he is to Audrey. After a lifetime spent with animal companions whose devotion and loyalty she never questioned, Occy's incredible journey has only strengthened Philippa's faith in the bond between humans and their pets.

'It just confirmed for me that animals, particularly dogs, are really remarkable. When they know they're loved, they will survive and they'll do whatever they need to do to get back to their family.'

Especially if it's a family like Occy's.

RUN, LU, RUN!

LUDIVINE'S STORY

Elkmont, Alabama, is one of those blink-and-you'll-miss-it kind of towns. Tucked away in the state's leafy, undulating north, an hour's drive from Alabama's fourth-largest city, Huntsville, and a stone's throw from the Tennessee state line, the tiny hamlet has just 450 residents. The downtown shopping strip boasts a total of six stores. It doesn't even have a traffic light.

Though rich in natural beauty, until recently Elkmont was arguably best known as the home of 1930s country music pioneers The Delmore Brothers, NFL star Michael Boley, and the award-winning Belle Chevre artisanal goat-cheese company.

But on 16 January 2016, everything changed. That was the day an inquisitive bloodhound called Ludivine went out for a walk and accidentally ran a half marathon – and Elkmont became headline news around the world.

Ludivine began her life in Alabama's largest prison. She was one of fourteen puppies born to Daisy, a purebred bloodhound, and Otis, a coonhound mix, at the Limestone Correctional Facility in the northern autumn of 2013. Located about 30 kilometres from Elkmont, between the towns of Athens and Harvest, Limestone houses more than 2000 male prisoners on 1600 acres of farmland, creeks and dense woodland – plenty of space for an enterprising inmate to try and secret contraband, or even himself. That's why the prison has an extensive dog-breeding program, raising and training beagles for use as contraband sniffer dogs and bloodhounds as people trackers.

April Hamlin, a guidance counsellor at Elkmont High School, had always wanted a 'hound dog'. Growing up, her grandfather bred coonhounds, which is the catch-all name for six distinct breeds of scent hound commonly used in raccoon hunting. 'When I was little I used to go out and sit in the pens with my grandfather's dogs. I've just always loved hound dogs,' April says.

As an adult, April always had at least one canine companion – 'usually mutts,' she laughs – before pledging her allegiance to the German shepherd when she married her husband, a long-time shepherd enthusiast. But the desire for a hound dog of her own never went away.

'I came to love German shepherds, but they need a job or they kind of go crazy. Once I had kids I didn't have as much time to spend with the dogs, and after our last German shepherd passed away a couple of years ago I said to my husband, "I'm getting a hound dog",' she explains. 'I wanted something that was a little bit less intense. I just wanted a lazy dog!'

April knew about the prison's breeding program, and asked a friend who worked there to give her a call if he ever had a bloodhound that wasn't cutting it as a tracking dog. He told April it was unlikely; they often rehomed beagle puppies that were surplus to prison requirements, but the bloodhound litters were less frequent, and all the puppies were usually drafted into service as trackers. He said she could have a beagle any time she liked, but April was willing to wait for her bloodhound.

A year later, she got the call. A six-week-old female bloodhound puppy had failed to pass muster and was looking for a new home.

The bloodhound is an ancient breed. It is believed to have originated in Belgium around 1000 AD, and the earliest references to them in English texts appeared in the thirteenth century. From the very beginning, bloodhounds have been used for tracking – originally deer and wild boar, and then from the Middle Ages, humans. A bloodhound can successfully follow a scent trail that is hours or even days old, across all manner of inhospitable terrain. In 1954, a bloodhound located the bodies of a missing Oregon family almost two weeks after they vanished.

The thing that makes bloodhounds such peerless tracking machines is, well, everything. Their long, pendulous ears drag on the ground when they're tracking, sweeping their quarry's skin cells and other scent particles into their nostrils. Their powerful neck and shoulder muscles mean they can keep their noses down, following a scent, over hundreds of kilometres and for long periods of time. Even the jowls that give them their permanent hangdog expression serve a purpose: known as the shawl, these loose skin folds also trap scent particles from the air and terrain.

But mostly, it's about the nose. The average dog's nose contains between 125 million and 220 million olfactory cells, or scent receptors. That's already forty times as many as humans; we have a comparatively paltry 5 million. But a bloodhound's nose has anywhere from 230 million to 300 million scent receptors. If the olfactory bulb – the part of the brain that analyses smells – in a human is the size of a postage stamp, in a bloodhound it's more like a handkerchief. These dogs are so adept at scent tracking that evidence procured by a bloodhound's nose is admissible in a court case.

Researchers believe bloodhounds actually 'see' scent. Sniffing a scent article – an item touched by their quarry, such as a piece of clothing or even a car seat – bombards their scent receptors, which then send a flurry of chemical messages to the olfactory bulb. This creates a highly detailed 'odour image' that helps the dog home in on breath, sweat and skin particles left behind by the subject. Once a bloodhound locks onto a scent trail, it won't stray from it regardless of how many other smells it encounters.

At least, that's the case with *most* bloodhounds. Ludivine, however, has always preferred to do things a little differently.

'They take these puppies when they're about five weeks old and put them out in the prison yard and just wait and see which ones look like they can track. They figure out which ones seem like they've got 'the gift' and they rehome the ones that don't,' says April. 'Ludivine was the first one they got rid of.'

Little Ludivine, it seemed, was a bit of a space cadet. A scatterbrain. A daydreamer. Adorable though she was, when they were handing out the essential skills for prison tracking dogs, easily distracted Lu must have been off chasing butterflies.

'They said she didn't have the attention span for it. She just did not have any focus at all, which is fine, but not for a tracking dog in a prison! My friend called and said, "We've got this one who's ready to go," so we went out to the prison and got her when she was six weeks old.'

Of course, Ludivine – pronounced loo-duh-veen – wasn't yet Ludivine. At the prison she hadn't had a name. It was up to the Hamlin family to choose a fitting moniker, so April delved into her ever-expanding file of potential pet names.

'Whenever I hear a name I'm always like, *That'd be a good name for a dog or a horse.* I'm always thinking that way,' she laughs.

She had recently seen the 2006 movie *A Good Year*, which stars Russell Crowe as an investment banker who inherits his uncle's chateau and vineyard in Provence. Along with the winery comes Ludivine Duflot, an eccentric housekeeper played by French actress Isabelle Candelier. The name seemed perfect for April's prison-yard punk puppy.

'The character is really kooky and crazy, and the name just seemed to fit. My kids were like, "Please don't name the dog Ludivine! We don't like that name." But I just said, "You can call her Lu!"'

As a lifelong dog owner who had never shied away from putting in the hours necessary to raise an obedient, well-behaved dog, April had imagined that training Lu would be a piece of cake. Bu as she set about schooling the new family member she quickly discovered that, while Ludivine may have lacked the tenacity required of a tracking dog, she definitely still had a stubborn streak.

'I'd read all this stuff about how hound dogs, after a certain point, just won't listen and I thought, *This won't be an issue for me*,' she says. 'But Ludivine spent a lot of time deciding she was not going to do what I said.'

She refused to come when called; in fact, she'd run in the opposite direction. She wouldn't walk on a leash. House-training took an eternity: Lu had the family's 40-acre farm at her disposal, but preferred to sneak off to the basement to relieve herself.

'The basement has a concrete floor, and she would run down there and go to the bathroom, I guess because she was used to the concrete floor in the prison kennel,' says April. 'We thought we'd never get her housebroken.'

But the whole family fell for quirky Ludivine nonetheless. 'I think she's beautiful. She has that noble bloodhound expression, and she's got a beautiful voice,' April says. 'She's goofy – she has absolutely no concept of personal space. She's the best dog to hug, she just leans in and melts into you. And she's really, really laid back.'

And after several frustrating months of zero progress on the training front, April finally stumbled upon Ludivine's weakness: pepperoni. Suddenly, the whip-smart pooch became much easier to handle. The family was even able to encourage Lu's tracking instincts in the 8-acre parcel of spring-fed woodland on their property.

'As she got bigger I'd take her for long walks around our farm, luring her with the pepperoni. I'll never forget the first time I took her into the woods. You could tell she was just like, *Wow, this is a whole new world*. My daughter, Thea, and son, Van, would take her out on a leash and I'd hide and she'd find me.'

But the fun tracking games evidently awakened something in Ludivine; something primal that she was powerless to resist. Suddenly, she wanted to roam. Since about the age of eighteen months, Lu has disappeared from April's property with predictable frequency. April will head off to work for the day, or simply let Ludivine outside to answer the call of nature (the toilet training finally having sunk in), and the dog will go on the lam, just like the prison escapees she was bred to track. On weekends, when Lu is set free to explore the whole property, she will invariably wander well beyond its boundaries.

Sometimes her journeys last just a few hours, and then Lu will come trotting happily home, no doubt having located whatever it was she'd set out to pursue. At other times, however, a sheepish April will have to go and retrieve her peripatetic puppy from wherever she's ended up.

'She'll find us wherever we are. My kids go to the school where I work, and Lu would come and find us there every day. They'd radio me and I'd have to take her home. She found us at the ball field once, too.'

The residents of sleepy Elkmont soon got to know and love the ebullient bloodhound as she made her rounds of the town. Sometimes they call April or text pictures to her: 'Lu's downtown, want me to bring her home?' Mostly, however, the locals leave her to her own devices, knowing she will find her way home before too long.

'Sometimes people who aren't from Elkmont will call and say, "I'm worried about your dog!" One lady picked her up and took her an hour away to Huntsville to keep her safe,' says April. 'Recently I had a guy call to say he'd spotted her and I said, "You know what, this sounds terrible but if you leave her alone she will be home in a few minutes." She's a bloodhound, she knows her way.'

Ludivine has regular haunts throughout Elkmont and its surrounds, but her favourite place to visit is the Richard Martin National Recreation Trail. The 16 kilometre trail is built on an abandoned rail corridor – hence its local nickname, Rails to Trails – and winds through downtown Elkmont, the Sulphur Trestle Fort site, and beautiful wetlands teeming with plants and animals native to the Tennessee Valley. It is named after Elkmont resident Richard Martin, who led community efforts to build the trail for twenty-five years.

Rails to Trails is popular with hikers, cyclists, runners, birdwatchers and horse riders – and Ludivine, who likes to join the trail downtown at Compton Street and lope alongside joggers or horses for as long as she pleases, or until she's halted and sent home by a well-meaning passerby. It also forms part of the route of Elkmont's annual half marathon, the Trackless Train Trek.

Well, the event *was* called the Trackless Train Trek for its inaugural running in 2016. From now on, however, it will be known as the Hound Dog Half, in recognition of its most famous participant, Ludivine.

The Trackless Train Trek was the brainchild of the parents and friends of Elkmont High School's young cross country and track athletes. Its aim was to raise money for the teams to be able to compete in events around the state.

'There are several parents and friends in the community who train with the kids in the summer and we enjoy getting together and running on the weekends. We enjoy the half marathon distance and realised that one was needed in

northern Alabama in January or February,' says race direc-
tor Gretta Armstrong.

As with virtually all long-distance running events and
community fun runs the world over, the Trackless Train
Trek had a strict 'no pets' policy. In fact, it wasn't even an
official policy; nobody thought to write it into the event's
terms and conditions, because nobody ever dreamed a two-
year-old bloodhound would take her place at the start line
alongside the 165 human competitors.

But that's exactly what happened. Ludivine strolled the
400 metres from April's front gate to downtown Elkmont
on January 16, no doubt following the tantalising scent
of the fresh coffee and bagels that runners were using to
fuel up and keep warm ahead of their race. And when the
starter's pistol fired promptly at 8 a.m. and everybody
started running, Lu ran right along with them.

'I did see Ludivine start the race and, to be honest, I was a
little concerned that she would get tangled up with the runners and cause someone to fall. The start of a race is always
crowded, and we were concerned about not only her safety,
but the safety of the other runners as well,' says Gretta. 'Fortunately, we had no tripping issues at the start of the race and
everybody got a chuckle when Lu started with the leaders.'

Like everyone else in Elkmont, Gretta knows Ludivine
well. 'Ludivine is a very, very sweet dog – she doesn't meet
a stranger, everyone is her friend. When you live in a
town with a population of 450, it isn't hard to know your
neighbours – even the four-legged ones!'

Once she saw the half marathon had begun without incident, Gretta got down to the important business of ensuring the rest of the race unfolded smoothly. She didn't give the bounding bloodhound another thought.

The first April knew of Ludivine's exploits on that chilly, grey Saturday morning was when a colleague from the high school who was volunteering at the half marathon sent her a picture of a proud-looking Lu wearing a finisher's medal around her neck. It was accompanied by a message: *Your dog just got seventh place in the half marathon!*

April chuckled. She hadn't realised Ludivine had even left the property. She figured Lu must have joined the race towards the end, maybe run the last few hundred metres, and the organisers had given her the medal for fun. April's biggest concern was that Ludivine might have been a hazard or got in the way of the real runners.

'My first thought was that Barry Pugh, the coach of the cross country and track teams, who I work with, was going to kill me! I didn't even go get her because I thought, *She'll come home*,' she recalls. 'Then I got another call from a friend saying, "You've got to get down here, people are going crazy over this dog."'

Only when she duly made her way downtown to collect her adventurous pet did April realise the true scale of Ludivine's incredible journey. She had run the *entire* half marathon – 21.1 kilometres or 13.1 miles – in an impressive time of 1:32:56. 'I just was not surprised at all,' April admits. 'She loves people, so she saw people running and just decided to run with them. What did surprise me was her focus. I've seen some pictures where she looks really serious.'

Gretta Armstrong, however, *was* surprised by Ludivine's feat. She was also unaware the dog had run the entire distance until she crossed the finish line. 'We are used to dogs joining us out [running] on the trail and then getting distracted, bored or tired and falling back, so for her to run the entire distance with the front of the pack is wonderfully awesome,' says Gretta.

'Coach Pugh and others working at the finish line were surprised when they saw her approaching, but it was only when Jim Clemens, who finished in fourth place, requested that they get her some water because "she ran the whole thing" that they realised that Lu had just run 13.1 miles.'

According to the official race results, Ludivine finished in a dead heat with fifty-year-old Jon Elmore, and was less than a minute behind the sixth placegetter, Huntsville's Tim Horvath. Lu was also three seconds faster than Julia Mateskon, also from Huntsville, which technically means she was the first female across the finish line. (For the record, the race was won by 38-year-old Keith Henry from Huntsville in a speedy 1:19:10.)

'I saw her for the first time in the parking lot before the race. She came bouncing up and I petted her on the head,' Tim Horvath told *Runner's World* magazine after the race. 'I saw her collar, so I just figured she was somebody's dog.

Elkmont is a small town where everyone knows everybody, so it didn't strike me as unusual.'

What did surprise him – and the rest of the field – was Lu's tenacity. She kept pace with the lead group of runners for most of the race, only slowing down or veering off the course when her nose led her somewhere more enticing. Three kilometres in, she paused to investigate a rabbit carcass. She also eschewed the aid stations manned by local volunteers in favour of rehydrating in a creek.

Every time she stopped, the lead runners thought Ludivine had had enough and would make her way home. But they didn't count on that infamous bloodhound bull-headed streak.

'One time she went over and met another dog next to the course. Later on, she went into a field with some mules and cows. Then she'd come back and run around our legs,' Tim told *Runner's World*. 'I wondered if she was going to get tired or go back to wherever her home was.'

No such luck. Ludivine may have been too easily distracted to make it as a prison tracking dog, but nothing was going to divert her from her goal that day – no doubt to the chagrin of the lead runners, who couldn't have banked on having to outrun a dog.

When she finished the half marathon, just like the rest of the runners, Ludivine slowed to a walk, 'like she knew, *I'm done*', says April. A kindly fellow participant offered her a slice of pizza, which Lu gratefully accepted – then raced away to bury it under a tree. As soon as April got her home, the exhausted hound curled up and went to sleep.

'She was very, very sleepy. We brought her home and she just passed out on the floor. She was still tired the next day, too,' she says.

If April imagined the story of Lu's half marathon adventure would remain a quirky local legend, she was in for another surprise. News of Ludivine's epic journey spread like wildfire. The tale was picked up by high-profile print, broadcast and online media outlets across the United States and Canada, and as far afield as the UK, Europe and Australia. She was invited to participate in a raft of fun runs near and far, and April set up a Twitter account and Facebook page for her that amassed nearly 2000 followers in just a month.

Ludivine was later named 'First Dog of Limestone County' and summoned to Elkmont Town Hall, where Limestone County Commission Chairman Mark Yarbrough presented her with another medal, this time for promoting the county and the town. Alabama Governor Robert Bentley even took to Twitter to congratulate Ludivine on her effort, and later wrote her a personal letter.

'It's been fun. We've had the best time with it, but I almost can't believe the reaction, because to me she's just Lu,' April says. 'Anyone who loves dogs just thinks it's the greatest thing. It's just a better story than what's usually on the news.'

April also discovered that Ludivine's remarkable run was apparently no fluke. 'I've had a lot of people contact me since saying, "She's run with me for so many miles on the Richard Martin Trail," so I think she was down there doing her training,' she laughs. 'When she's out roaming there's no telling how far she goes.'

The Trackless Train Trek was renamed the Hound Dog Half in Lu's honour and organisers made t-shirts emblazoned with her image. They are sold at local events and online to raise money for Elkmont High School's cross country and track teams.

For Gretta Armstrong, renaming the race was a no-brainer. 'Ludivine's story went viral and travelled around the world. We were inundated with requests for information, pictures, and interviews, and since this race is a fundraiser for the kids, we want to do all we can to keep the momentum going,' she says. 'We discussed it with April before we renamed the race and she was all for it.'

April says she has no desire to personally gain from Lu's global celebrity, but she's thrilled that her singular, goofy dog is now in a position to make a difference. 'I haven't done anything – I just opened the door one Saturday morning and let the dog out – but it did happen, and I think it happened for a reason. Now we want to use her fame for charitable purposes.'

People often ask April what she imagines Ludivine was thinking as she ran and ran and ran that day, and she's convinced she knows the answer.

'I really have thought about it, and I'm sure I know what she was thinking. Somewhere in that race I think she consciously decided she was going to run the rest of it. She would have thought she was having the best time, and so she just kept going,' she says. 'She was thinking, *I'm out here, and all these people are here to see me. I'm free.'*

It's amazing what can happen when you just follow your nose.

AROUND THE WORLD IN 80 WAYS

OSCAR'S STORY

There are taller and wider waterfalls in the world, but none produces a curtain of falling water larger or more spectacular than Africa's Victoria Falls. At the height of the rainy season in March and April, more than 500 million cubic metres of water per minute plummets over the edge of the 1.7-kilometre-wide falls, which form the border between Zambia and Zimbabwe on the Zambesi River, into a gorge more than 100 metres below. Columns of spray rise nearly a kilometre into the air and can be seen from up to 50 kilometres away.

The area's indigenous Tokaleya people named the falls Mosi-oa-Tunya – 'the smoke that thunders' – and it's easy to see why. That primal, thundering beauty is also undeniably dangerous. In recent years, a number of tourists have reportedly slipped to their deaths from the so-called 'Devil's Pool', a natural infinity pool on the edge of the falls on the Zambian side.

The breathtaking scenery of the falls is matched only by the abundance and array of wildlife in the national parks that surround it. The parks are home to large populations of elephants, buffalo, zebras, monkeys, baboons and giraffes, with lions, leopards and cheetahs also regularly spotted.

The Zambesi itself is teeming with hippopotamuses and crocodiles, both of which have deservedly fearsome reputations, and rightly so – hippos alone are purportedly responsible for more human deaths in Africa each year than lions, elephants, leopards, buffalo and rhinoceroses combined. The hotels that line the riverbanks have installed electric fencing to keep the creatures, which are well known for their aggression, from menacing the guests.

Awe-inspiring though it may be, the powerful and potentially deadly Victoria Falls is perhaps not the ideal spot for a little dog to take a twilight swim. But that's just what happened one night in May 2009, when a five-year-old bitser called Oscar decided to take a dip.

Zambia was the latest stop for Oscar and his owner, Joanne Lefson, on a round-the-world trip. Joanne was relaxing outside her hotel with a drink after a long day of travelling when the evening took a terrifying turn. She thought Oscar was in his usual position at her feet, but he had slipped away.

'The next moment the security guards were going crazy. Oscar had gotten through the gates somehow and was swimming in the river, two hundred metres from Victoria Falls,' she recalls. 'Wherever there was water he'd be straight in there because he loved swimming.'

Joanne ran to the water's edge and screamed his name over the roar of the water. Oscar paddled on, oblivious to the fact that 'there were thousands of crocodiles' eyeing him up as a tasty snack. 'I thought,' says Joanne, 'that there was no way he was going to get back.'

All she could do was stare out into the darkness and pray.

Oscar and Joanne's global odyssey had officially begun that May, when they left Joanne's native South Africa on what she had dubbed the 'World Woof Tour'. In reality, however, their journey began in January 2004, when Joanne returned to Cape Town from San Diego following the end of her marriage to an American veterinarian.

She had a new home and was embarking on a new life, but Joanne felt something was missing. A passionate dog-lover all her life, she knew it was time for a new canine companion.

'It's hard to say exactly when and where my love of dogs started, but I did always have a dog in my life,' she says. Her father had enjoyed an idyllic *Passage to India*-style childhood. Growing up with his British parents in India under British rule, he had kept elephants and peacocks as pets, but Joanne 'was always drawn to dogs growing up'.

'My parents were divorced, so I think whatever family dog we had at the time became a constant in the family – a loving being that never changed,' she says.

As soon as she was old enough, Joanne signed up as a volunteer at the local Society for the Prevention of Cruelty to Animals (SPCA) shelter. 'Eventually my parents banned me because they said, "Every time you go to volunteer you bring another dog back." Maybe I was a dog in a past life, I don't know!'

But while her vocation was temporarily delayed, her experiences at the shelter proved formative for Joanne. Day after day, as she saw neglected, abused and unwanted dogs dumped at the shelter or picked up as strays, she says she developed a soft spot for life's underdogs – both the literal and figurative varieties.

'I remember a little puppy being euthanised when I was twelve or thirteen, and to see something go from being so healthy and alive to simply not being there within seconds, I was like, *How can this happen?*' she says. 'That was a big emotional connection for me, and it never really left me.'

She was baffled by what she saw as a general belief that shelter dogs were 'damaged goods' when all she was seeing was healthy, intelligent, affectionate canines that simply wanted a chance. 'People's perception was that only "bad" dogs are available at shelters and it was so frustrating for me. Shelter dogs are such amazing creatures and they're so overlooked,' she says.

Joanne later earned a degree in wildlife and fisheries science from Texas A&M University and established a career as a professional golfer and journalist. But even after her marriage and a move to the United States, the plight of shelter dogs was never far from her thoughts. 'The reason I married a vet was I figured I could save on a few bills for the animal shelters I was involved with,' she laughs.

So when she went home to South Africa after her divorce in 2004, a trip to the SPCA's Cape of Good Hope shelter in Grassy Park was high on her to-do list. As a veteran dog adopter – she had welcomed at least a dozen 'second chance' canines into her home over the years – Joanne had always made a point of rescuing the dogs others dismissed. 'I'd always take the oldest or the ugliest or the one I thought had no chance,' she says.

She had already shortlisted a couple of dogs that fit the bill on that January day when she passed by kennel B5. In it sat a sturdy little mutt with a scruffy brindle coat, floppy ears and a wide doggy grin. He had been picked up as a stray and didn't even have a name; shelter staff simply referred to him by the number on his cage.

'I had a friend with me and we just started laughing because he was so funny looking. He rolled over on his back and he was just so cute,' Joanne says.

Beguiling as he was, Joanne discounted the little dog as a potential pet. He was completely adorable and was sure to find a home quickly; she was set on choosing a dog that wasn't blessed with such good looks. 'I thought, *I can't take the cutest dog at the pound*,' she says.

But fate can be capricious, especially for dogs in shelters. This appealing canine may have been the cutest dog at the pound, but he had already been there for twelve days. At the SPCA, stray dogs that are not reclaimed within ten days are made available for adoption. Many are adopted quickly; those that are not can languish in the shelter for months or even years. Some dogs don't cope in the shelter environment and develop a psychological condition known as 'kennel stress', which can manifest as panting, pacing, aggression or depression. In these cases, the SPCA's policy is that the kindest option is euthanasia.

If the friendless creature didn't find a home soon, his future could be grim indeed. 'In that moment I decided, *Okay, I'll take him*,' says Joanne. She named him Oscar.

Because he was a stray, the shelter had no information about Oscar's life before Joanne adopted him. They didn't even know his age or breed; their best guess was that he was about a year old, and he looked like a terrier mix. (Years later Joanne had Oscar DNA tested by a Florida laboratory, and the results revealed his genetic make-up was a mix of Alsatian, corgi and bassett hound.) What was in no doubt was just how *cute* Oscar was. Everywhere she went with her new four-legged friend, Joanne was mobbed by people who wanted to know where she had found such a charming little dog.

'From day one, he just attracted so much attention,' she says. 'I'd just been looking for a buddy to hang out with, but it didn't matter whether I was at a coffee shop or driving in the car, people would say, "What kind of dog is this?" or "Where can I get one like him?" I could have given him away a hundred times a day.'

By 2007, three years after Joanne had adopted Oscar, people were still asking. Oscar's unusual appearance led most inquirers to ask if he was a purebred, some new breed that had cornered the market in 'adorable'. Their inevitable surprise when Joanne explained that she had rescued Oscar from her local shelter was disheartening.

'Every time I said, "He's from a shelter," the reaction was the same. It was like, "No way, you don't get nice dogs from shelters,"' she recalls.

According to Joanne, dog adoption rates in South Africa are about 7 per cent, meaning less than one dog is adopted for every ten that find themselves in shelters. It was clear to Joanne that shelter dogs had an image problem in her home country. She felt compelled to do something about it and knew that Oscar would be the key.

'I was thinking, *How can I use this amazing, cute, friendly being to really challenge people's perception of what goes on in shelters?* Who better than a shelter dog to champion that cause?'

The more she thought about it, and the more she researched, the more Joanne realised that low adoption rates were not a uniquely South African problem. Shelter dogs are seen by many as an inferior alternative to puppies bought from breeders or purchased in pet shops all around the world. For example in her second home, America, almost 4 million dogs enter shelters each year, and more than a million of those are ultimately euthanised. If she could only introduce delightful Oscar to as many people as possible, Joanne felt she could start to change people's minds about adopting dogs from shelters.

A seed of an idea began to germinate in her mind. She loved to travel. Why couldn't she and Oscar visit those countries with low pet adoption rates? Why couldn't Oscar prove to the whole world what an amazing companion a shelter dog can be?

'Somewhere in the mix of all those things I thought, *We need to go around the world*,' says Joanne.

And just like that, the World Woof Tour (WWT) was born.

In early 2008, Joanne started planning Oscar's and her global tour in earnest. She mapped out a route, selecting countries based on a range of factors including ease of travel, the number of animal shelters there, and the likelihood of being able to arrange media coverage. The mission would be pointless, she knew, unless she could draw attention to the issues she and Oscar were aiming to highlight. Other destinations were added to the itinerary simply because Joanne felt they couldn't be missed. 'In Turkey we wanted to visit a specific shelter that had over three thousand dogs, just to believe it,' she says.

The WWT would be mostly overland. Joanne wanted to limit the amount of air travel because she felt uncomfortable about Oscar having to travel alone in the hold of an aircraft. There would, of course, have to be some long-haul flights but Joanne tried not to dwell on her jitters as she penciled them in.

Once she had mapped out her dream itinerary, Joanne had a list of thirty-seven countries she and Oscar would visit. 'I literally just called a company that does animal transport services and said, "Here's the route, is this actually possible?" They came back and said there would be quite a bit of paperwork involved, but yes, it would be doable.'

Joanne admits she didn't spend a lot of time thinking about restrictions such as quarantine when planning the journey. Consequently, some parts of the WWT had to be rejigged. 'We had to take out one or two countries, like Japan and Australia. All the island countries were going to be a problem, because if one disease comes onto an island it will spread really quickly,' she explains.

For the most part, travel between nations would be relatively straightforward, though in some countries complex paperwork would be required.

By May 2009, after fourteen months of virtually full-time planning, Joanne and Oscar were ready to depart.

By the time the intrepid pair reached Victoria Falls, they were well and truly in the swing of their adventure. They had seen so many incredible sights already – Joanne names Namibia, the third stop on the WWT, as one of the journey's highlights – and she simply couldn't believe her luck.

'To have the privilege and the opportunity to travel around the world with my best buddy was a dream come true. I was just so grateful I had the funds, I had my best friend, and we were able to do it,' she says. 'There wasn't one day that I didn't wake up going, *How cool is this?* I think Oscar was the same. We would look at each other like, "What are we doing?"'

But as she stood on the banks of the Zambesi River, howling Oscar's name into the darkness, Joanne felt it was all unravelling before her eyes.

Miraculously, Oscar *did* make it back to shore, ambling out of the fast-flowing river in his own good time. He was unscathed and unfazed by all the fuss, but it was a 'serious reality check', Joanne says – a milestone moment in a journey that had until that point been all about fun, friendship and making a difference.

'I realised then that it was not a party, and that I was really going to have to think about things,' she says. 'I still get goosebumps when I think about how a split second here or there could have meant a totally different outcome.'

The WWT rolled on. Joanne and Oscar went to Cambodia – 'a stunning country filled with happy people and happy dogs,' she says – Greece, France, Malaysia. They rode together on the Peter Pan's Flight ride at Disneyland in Los Angeles. They even trekked to Machu Picchu, the mysterious Incan citadel set high in the Andes mountains in Peru.

Another highlight was getting 'married' in Las Vegas. An Elvis impersonator officiated, and Joanne and Oscar vowed to promote dog adoption until death do them part. 'I wasn't even the first one to do it. I was part of a long tradition of people that had married their llamas and all sorts,' she laughs.

It was not always easy. Oscar's presence in China, for example, was controversial and the travel company advised Joanne to enlist a local 'fixer'-cum-bodyguard to ensure their safety. The Chinese capital, Beijing, implemented a one-dog policy in 2006 that restricts residents to owning a single pet dog. More than forty breeds are banned in the city, including Dalmatians, Australian shepherds, greyhounds and boxers. Dogs must be under 35.5 centimetres tall – Oscar was larger – and owners cannot take their pets to public places such as markets, parks and tourist sites.

Joanne bristled at the limitations, and defied the regulations by taking Oscar to the Great Wall of China. It was risky – 'China has zero tolerance; if you break the rules, that's it,' she says – but they pulled it off.

Malaysia also proved challenging. Joanne and Oscar were booked on a ferry to the island of Langkawi when at the last moment officials denied Oscar passage. It was crucial the pair boarded the boat in order to continue on to Thailand.

'The boat was leaving so I basically just threw Oscar in at the last minute and hoped they wouldn't throw us off once we'd started the journey,' Joanne says. 'Often we didn't have a choice. We always got our way in the end, but sometimes it was a bit more challenging. There were moments when we didn't know how it was going to work out and it was a matter of doing what needed to be done without any risk to Oscar's safety.'

There was another terrifying experience in Croatia when Oscar and Joanne got separated and he disappeared. He was finally spotted an hour and a half later, nose to the ground, as if trying to sniff his way back to his mistress.

'I'll never forget the look he gave me. It was as if he was saying, "That was close. We shouldn't be doing that again,"' she says. 'He knew we'd almost lost each other and we were totally on the same page after that.'

Joanne and Oscar maintained a blistering pace throughout their tour. They stayed in each destination for just a couple of days, squeezing in as many visits to shelters and photo opportunities at iconic locations as possible before moving on. 'It wasn't a vacation, we were on a mission,' she says, though they did linger for longer in northern India, where Joanne had co-founded a donkey sanctuary in Ladakh years earlier, and California, where she had lived for many years.

It was tiring, too, but Oscar handled the trek with his customary aplomb. 'Dogs get jet lag for sure,' Joanne laughs. 'When I was tired, he was tired. Oscar was the priority, so if he was tired we would sleep.'

The people they met often asked Joanne if she believed Oscar knew what was happening. Did he appreciate the fact that he was making his way around the world, seeing things that many humans can only dream of? Joanne is certain the little dog understood the magnitude of their quest.

'Oscar knew that we were going to different places and he reacted differently depending on the circumstances. He was interested and curious,' she says. 'We rode a camel in the desert in India. He met a manatee on the Amazon. He loved Kalimantan, the Indonesian portion of the island of Borneo – he was a monkey fanatic so he loved the monkeys there.'

And Joanne's fears about Oscar having to travel in air-craft holds proved largely unfounded – the little dog was such a novelty that he was allowed to travel in the cabin with Joanne on almost every flight they took. It was a good thing, because on the rare occasions he *was* in the hold, Joanne proved a high-maintenance passenger.

'On the flight from Moscow to Delhi I was saying to the cabin crew every twenty minutes, "I want to know the tem-perature in the hold!" Eventually they said, "If we show you your dog in the hold, will you shut up?"' she laughs. 'We went to the back of the plane where there was a hatch you could open and go into the hold. There was Oscar, abso-lutely fine.'

She realised then that Oscar didn't need a window seat and a view. He didn't need luxury hotels, gourmet meals or any of the other trappings of travel that many humans deem essential. All he needed was Joanne.

'As long as we were together, it was great,' she says. 'We were a complete team.'

Joanne and Oscar completed the World Woof Tour in December 2009. Their journey had taken them to forty-two countries in all – the thirty-seven on their original itinerary plus another five they visited after the end of the official tour. They returned to South Africa and life largely went back to normal. Joanne resumed her work as a journalist, writing for golf magazines. She also wrote a book about their odyssey, *Ahound the World: My Travels with Oscar.*

But the travel bug had well and truly bitten, and in the years that followed Joanne began yearning for a new journey with her best friend. The World Woof Tour had drawn an enormous amount of media attention to the plight of shelter dogs worldwide, but she wanted to show even more people what these second-chance dogs were really capable of.

So she decided that she and Oscar would trek to Mount Everest's South Base Camp in Nepal, 5364 metres above sea level. 'The idea was to strongly market dog adoption again, because the problem didn't magically go away after the World Woof Tour,' says Joanne.

But they would never make it to the mountain together.

Joanne and Oscar had been spending an increasing amount of time in the US, though South Africa was still home. On January 11, 2013, they were in San Jose, California, just a couple of weeks away from returning to Cape Town to complete the final arrangements for their Base Camp expedition.

Tragically, Joanne bumped Oscar with her car. He could not be saved, and her world fell apart. She still struggles to talk about that terrible day.

'It was an accident. I still don't even know how it happened,' she says. 'It's been a nightmare. From that moment my perspective changed. I woke up a different person. He was my soulmate. Every day I appreciated what we had.'

She returned to South Africa and spent months asking, *Why?* Friends encouraged her to adopt another dog, not to replace Oscar but to continue what he had started. She couldn't bring herself to contemplate it. Oscar, she felt, had been born to do the World Woof Tour; born to 'give his buddies in shelters a voice'.

'There wasn't a day that I didn't get an email from someone saying, *I've got this amazing dog that I adopted because of Oscar's story,*' she says. 'It moved me. Every life counts, and if our tour saved one life it was worth it. Every dog saved was an Oscar. The point is that a dog really can change your life.'

Gradually, Joanne began to emerge from the fog of her grief. She realised how lucky she was to have had him and felt that Oscar's journey could – and should – continue. She just wasn't sure how.

She retreated to India to mull it over, and there, just as it had with Oscar, fate intervened once again.

Mumbai filmmaker Dev Agarwal had approached Joanne, seeking to make a documentary about the donkey sanctuary. She took him to shoot some footage at a dump where one of the sanctuary's donkeys had been found.

'This little puppy just came straight up to me and collapsed at my feet,' she says.

The puppy was around eight months old, starving and extremely dehydrated. Joanne knew he was mere hours from death. In the past, she might have taken the tiny dog in, but still raw from the loss of Oscar, she just didn't have the heart. Instead, she took the puppy back to the sanctuary where the caretaker, Sonam Angchuk, took him in. He named the dog Rupee and nursed him back to health.

Meanwhile, Joanne went back to Cape Town with a new goal: to open her own dog shelter. It had been a long-held dream, but one that had been put on the backburner in the wake of the World Woof Tour. After Oscar's death, Joanne says she felt a renewed urgency to tell the world just how special shelter dogs are.

She bought a rural property at Franschhoek, 75 kilometres east of Cape Town – she actually found the property within a week of his passing and took it as a sign she was on the right path – and opened Oscar's Arc in October 2016.

'Oscar and I travelled around the world and we were hanging out and having an okay time, but there was more we could have been doing,' Joanne says. 'I would give up everything to have him back again, but losing him made me wake up again. I miss him every day and I do look back and think, *I wish*, but in going forwards with everything I'm doing now I'm honouring him, because he still drives everything that I do.'

While Oscar's Arc is a working shelter, Joanne says the broader aim is to continue to challenge people's misconceptions and encourage them to adopt from their own local shelters. Its innovations include offering 'name your price' adoptions and providing free dog training for every adopted dog. 'We're a shelter but we look like a six-star resort,' she says of the innovative facility. 'The bigger picture is to radically challenge people's perceptions of what shelter dogs are. Oscar's legacy is to inspire people to think, *We want a dog, let's go to a shelter.*'

By not looking like a typical shelter, Joanne also hopes Oscar's Arc will reach people who claim they can't face going to a shelter because 'it's too sad'.

'Know that when you go there you're part of the change. You're picking out one dog that doesn't have to be there anymore. It's a life saved, and that's so powerful,' she says. 'Oscar and I saw some amazing shelters on our travels. Some were sad, but most were brilliant and inspiring and filled with people who truly care about these animals and work so damn hard for them.'

While it still feels like yesterday for Joanna that Oscar died, in the years since the accident she has chosen to focus on the incredible journey she and Oscar shared – not just the World Woof Tour, but the entire nine years they spent together.

'He was an amazing dog, and I feel very lucky that I got him. Every single dog that I've ever adopted was an amazing dog that brought so much into my life and set every-thing up for me going forward,' she says. 'A lot of people have their own Oscar, and when it passes away they don't want to get another because they can't replace that dog. I'm never going to find another Oscar, but I might find a Rufus or a Charlie . . .'

Or a Rupee. Several months after rescuing him from the dump, Joanne returned to India and brought Rupee home to South Africa. She couldn't shake the idea that she was supposed to take a shelter dog on the journey to Everest Base Camp, even if that dog couldn't be Oscar. Who better than a dog that hailed from Ladakh, a city more than 3000 metres above sea level in the Himalaya?

In November 2013, Joanne and Rupee left the town of Lukla in Nepal and trekked for a gruelling ten days to reach Base Camp, accompanied by Dev Agarwal, who was film-ing their journey. Joanne had hired an extra porter to carry Rupee if he needed it, but the plucky mountain dog rose to the challenge. He is believed to be the first dog officially recorded at Base Camp.

Now three, Rupee is quite at home in South Africa with Joanne. He's not Oscar, but that's okay.

'Rupee has been a challenge, but what I've learned is that you can't make a dog how you want it to be. Every dog is an individual, just like a person,' she says. 'Rupee is from a place where they don't keep dogs as pets, so it was a steep learning curve for him. But he got a chance. There is no better dog than an adopted dog.'

So much of Joanne's journey – and Oscar's and Rupee's – she believes was written in the stars. The fact that Oscar shared his name with a certain gold statuette awarded to film stars isn't lost on her. 'I picked a dog I wouldn't normally have chosen, that probably wouldn't have been there the next day because the threat of euthanasia was ever present,' she says. 'Talk about a star dog that came from nothing and really did something.'

Oscar's Arc is now her mission, and beyond that, who knows? What Joanne does know is that, wherever the stars lead her next, Oscar will be there to guide her.

INTO THE FIRE

BONNIE'S STORY

The heat was unbearable. The flames were still 300 metres away, but they advanced like a tidal wave, causing the old ute's paint job to bubble and blister.

John stomped on the accelerator pedal and desperately twisted the key in the ignition. Finally, mercifully, the ute came growling to life. He clipped the gatepost as he sped out of the driveway and turned right into Sturt Road. It was a dead end, but he knew there was a farm at the end of the road that had a dam. John would plunge the car straight into it if he had to.

On the passenger seat his dog, Bonnie, was trembling. She didn't know what was happening any more than John did. Was it a terrorist attack? Was somebody dropping bombs? Going by the roar that surrounded them, and the boom of distant explosions, anything seemed possible.

He floored it, careering blindly into the choking black smoke. Then – *BANG!* The ute hit something in the road with such force the windscreen popped out and shattered. John's first thought was for Bonnie. Thank the Lord above she was still in one piece.

John tried the engine once, twice, three times. Nothing.

They were surrounded by fire now. Great towering walls of flame bore down on their mangled vehicle. The inferno was like a living thing, a predator toying with its prey. John clambered out of the car, Bonnie close at his heels with her leash trailing behind her. Through the smoke haze, he could now just about make out what he'd hit. The dim outline of a massive gum tree stretched across the road, its trunk dancing with embers, its bark black and charred.

John crouched down low and tried to seek shelter by shimmying under the car, but the road might as well have been the surface of the sun. It was so hot the bitumen had begun to melt. He raced to the shoulder of the road, grabbed a big stick, tried to jam it into the earth. If he could dig a hole and cover himself and Bonnie in soil, perhaps they could survive this unrelenting, incandescent heat.

But the dirt was too hard – and where was Bonnie? John looked frantically for her, peering into the smoke, his good eye feeling gritty and singed. There she was, a couple of metres away, her white coat now soot black. She turned and looked at John, then darted in the opposite direction.

'Bonnie!' he shouted, hearing the fear in his own voice. She stopped and he took off in pursuit. But the moment he had her within arm's reach, she skittered away again.

What was she playing at? She was heading back towards the house, and a glance in that direction told John there wasn't likely to be anything left of it. He shouted her name again, and again she stopped. John went after her once more, and once more she turned and ran. This went on and on. Every time John got close to Bonnie, she would journey further away.

He was struggling to breathe now. The fire was sucking all the oxygen from the air. The heat was maddening, and he was so tired. He tried to follow Bonnie again, but something grabbed him around the legs and he fell. He didn't know what had him; couldn't see it through the smoke. He kicked and struggled with the meagre energy he had left.

Barbed wire, brought down by the trees crashing to earth all around him. John extricated himself as quickly as he could then staggered to his feet. He looked for Bonnie but couldn't see her.

'Bonnie!' he yelled. 'Come on, girl!'

But all he could hear was the crackle and hiss of the flames. There was no sign of his dog. Bonnie had been swallowed by the smoke.

John Laffan is a man of faith. He has faith in the inherent goodness of people; faith in human beings' capacity for change. As a volunteer Salvation Army chaplain, he has faith in God, too, though he's not evangelical about it. But above all else, John has faith in dogs. Of all the challenges he has surmounted in his sixty-three years – from being partially blinded by his own father, to substance abuse and homelessness – only one inspires him to use the word 'miracle', and it was a miracle performed by a diminutive kelpie–blue heeler cross called Bonnie.

The way John and Bonnie came together was something of a miracle in itself. For eighteen years, John had shared his life with a wire-haired terrier mix called Patches. He paid $10 for her in a pet shop, mere hours before she was going to be dumped – or worse – by the shop's owners, who had deemed her unsellable. A couple of years later his marriage ended, and Patches became John's constant companion.

John hasn't had an easy life. As a toddler, a beating by his alcoholic father cost him the sight in one eye. He has been destitute and homeless. He slept rough on the streets of Melbourne for five years, and is recovered from substance abuse himself. He receives a disability pension due to his blindness, and has never had much money. But despite, or perhaps because of, his many trials, John realised long ago that his purpose is to help others.

'I made a choice when I was very young that I wanted to serve humanity. There are more precious things in life than money. That's not where your wealth is,' he says.

John lived at Kinglake, a mountain town 50 kilometres north-east of Melbourne in the Kinglake Ranges, part of the

Great Dividing Range, but joined the Salvos and started ministering to Melbourne's inner-city homeless community, as well as working in prisons and with drug and alcohol services – all with little Patches by his side.

'I had a caravan that I'd converted into a soup kitchen, and I'd feed homeless people in the street out of my own pocket. Patches used to come out with me on Friday and Saturday nights. She was such a friendly, beautiful little dog.'

Sadly, Patches was diagnosed with lymphatic cancer in the late 1990s, and John was forced to make the heart-breaking decision to have her put to sleep. For more than five years, he couldn't bring himself to contemplate ever having another dog. Then, one day in 2004, the choice was taken out of his hands.

In his Salvation Army capacity, John had been working with a family heavily affected by substance abuse who were facing eviction from their rented home in the northern Melbourne suburb of Mill Park. One day he arrived at the property to find the police and RSPCA officers in attendance. They had been called in response to a wild party the night before, during which several puppies and kittens in the family's care had been killed.

Only one dog had survived, but she had been the victim of horrific cruelty and was in a bad way. John guessed she was under twelve months old, but she was clearly mal-nourished and so underweight it was impossible to determine her exact age. She had virtually no fur and her frail body was covered in cigarette burns. She was bleeding from her ears and rectum, indicating internal injuries.

In an instant, John knew the little dog was meant for him. 'When I was a kid growing up, animals were more friends to me than people were. I found acceptance amongst the animals,' he explains. 'They mean a lot to me, and if I can help a few and save a few while I'm on this planet, so be it.'

He asked the RSPCA officers if he could adopt the dog. 'They were about to give her the "green dream" (the euthanasia drug pentobarbital). I begged them not to, but they said, "She won't last a week, it's kinder to put her down now,"' he recalls. 'Even if she did survive, they said she'd be aggressive, that she'd never come around.'

They were also concerned that her internal organs may not have developed properly, he says, as she had never received adequate nutrition. Neighbours of the family later revealed to John the scale of their cruelty: they would offer the dog food, then beat her when she tried to take it.

Though the dog's prognosis was grim, John would not be dissuaded. He pleaded for the puppy's life, vowed to get her the best veterinary care, and eventually the RSPCA officers relented.

He named the dog Bonnie, took her home to Kinglake and duly delivered her to the local vet, who promptly burst into tears. She was able to diagnose the full extent of Bonnie's injuries, which included three broken ribs and a punctured lung.

'She also said Bonnie wouldn't last a week, but I took her home and nursed her back to health. A month went by and she was getting better,' John says.

In the early days of her recuperation, it seemed all Bonnie did was eat. She would catch and eat rodents, because she had grown used to scavenging whatever nourishment she could find. John left her largely to her own devices, never forcing her to interact or putting her on public display.

'I just let her do her own thing. She'd sleep under the bed, where she felt safe, and watch me working, going in and out of the house,' he says. 'There were a number of different moments where I knew in my heart she was coming around. I'd be sitting at the end of the bed and she'd jump up and stick her head under my arm, or I'd go to the toilet and she'd come in and sit between my feet. Slowly she began to follow me around.'

As she grew stronger and gained weight, John also started to see what a 'pretty little thing' Bonnie was. Her working-dog heritage was obvious in her appearance, but she certainly didn't have the boisterous temperament of a cattle dog. Bonnie was quiet, passive, content to spend her days by the side of the only person in the world that she trusted.

More than a decade later, John still doesn't quite know why he insisted on taking gravely ill Bonnie home with him from Mill Park that day, but feels that somehow her spirit spoke to him. She let him know she was bigger and braver than her broken little body suggested.

'I think it was just the look in her eyes,' he says. 'I think animals have a sense about people, and she must have sensed something about me that she felt safe with.'

Like Patches before her, Bonnie seemed to empathise with the homeless and struggling people John worked with. She was unfailingly gentle and patient with them, and appeared to feel comfortable in their company.

The so-called 'inevitable' aggression John had been warned about materialised only once. A couple John had been working with managed to find his home address and paid an unexpected visit.

'He was into ice [methamphetamine] and wanted money [for drugs]. I said, "No, I can help you with other stuff, but not that." He punched me in the face and I fell backwards onto the floor,' says John. 'Bonnie leapt up and ripped his leg open.'

The man threatened to kill both John and Bonnie before eventually departing. Half an hour later the local police sergeant arrived to investigate the man's allegation of a dog attack.

'I told him what had happened and he reached over and patted Bonnie on the head and said, "Good girl, more power to you. You look after your old dad."'

That was the first time Bonnie saved John's life. It wouldn't be the last.

Victoria's Black Saturday bushfires were the worst in Australian history. In the course of one horrific day, as many as 400 individual fires tore through 1.1 million acres of land and razed 3500 structures, including more than 2000 homes. The bushfires also claimed 173 lives – Australia's highest ever loss of life from a bushfire disaster – and injured a further 414 people. Along with Marysville, an hour east, Kinglake was one of the towns affected the worst, with 38 people killed and more than 500 homes destroyed.

But when Saturday, 7 February 2009, dawned in Kinglake, there was no indication of the terror and destruction that was to come. It was oppressively hot, but that was nothing new for this time of year. For the past week, temperatures had hovered around the 40°C mark right across Victoria, and on 30 January the mercury had tipped 45°C in Melbourne – the third hottest day in the city's history. It was windy, too, with gusts of up to 125 km/hr.

John had been one of Kinglake's 1500-odd residents for around twenty years. He was used to the extreme weather that often enveloped the town, from deep snow in winter to these sweltering summer days. But even for John, 7 February was a warm one. So warm, in fact, that he cancelled plans to meet friends at a country music festival in the town of Whittlesea, 25 kilometres to the west. His ute kept overheating in the sizzling conditions, and he was tired, having tossed and turned in the heat all through the previous night. So he decided to stay home and potter around his old rented farmhouse, trying to keep himself and Bonnie as cool as possible.

Around 4 p.m., John's mobile phone suddenly died. He replaced the battery, but it made no difference; the phone was kaput. He tried the landline, but it was dead, too.

Then he heard a chilling howling on the wind.

'I went outside and the whole sky had just turned black, and the sun was blood red. I could hear this roar in the distance that sounded like a jet aircraft or a massive train,' he says. 'All sorts of things went through my head. I honestly thought somebody had dropped a bomb. I didn't realise it was a bushfire, because I'd never been in one.'

Save for his faithful companion Bonnie, John was alone on the property, which was about 5 kilometres from the town itself and surrounded by dense bush. With his phones out of use, he had no connection to the outside world. His nearest neighbours were almost a kilometre away through the bush. He went back outside into the eerie, dark afternoon and turned on the radio in the ute.

'There was a bit of crackling, then finally I heard something about a bushfire coming. They said there was a remote possibility that Kinglake might come under "ember attack",' he recalls. 'I didn't know that half of Kinglake had already been destroyed by four o'clock.'

What John did know, however, was that staying put would be suicidal. His first instinct was to shelter in an old water tank next to the house, but he quickly dismissed the idea. Even if he could haul himself up a ladder to the top, how would he get Bonnie up there? And there was a

3.5 metre drop down into the tank; how would they get out again?

There was only one realistic chance of survival. He had to make a break for it. 'I grabbed Bonnie and a biscuit tin full of family photos and got in the car. I had a terrible, terrible time trying to get the car going. The fire was just sucking the oxygen away from everything. I saw trees go up [in flames], sheds go up. Half the roof had come off the house. The windows had blown in.'

He could see flames now, advancing up the hill towards his home like some demonic army. There was a gully at the end of the street; it was a sea of fire. Panic rose like bile in John's throat. If he was going to make it to Kinglake, he would have to drive into that gully.

When he finally got the car going, he drove in the opposite direction instead, towards a dead end where there was a farm with a dam. 'I thought there'd be safety in numbers,' he explains.

But safety remained frighteningly out of reach. In the almost impenetrable smoke haze, John's ute smashed into a fallen tree. He abandoned the car and frantically searched for salvation in the burning bush. As he worked to dig a hole at the side of the road, his mobile phone began vibrating in his back pocket, having reconnected with the intermittent signal.

'I pulled it out of my pocket and put it to my ear and heard a voice I didn't recognise say, "John, start praying."'

But John didn't pray. He couldn't. He is a devout Christian, but in that moment he couldn't see how God could help him. There didn't seem to be a way out. 'At that point,' he says, 'it came down to human will to survive.'

That's when Bonnie began her game of 'catch me if you can', repeatedly disappearing into the smoke and flame, then returning to hover anxiously just beyond John's grasp.

'She was stopping and looking back at me, but as soon as I got anywhere near her she'd turn and run back into the bush,' he says. Then the penny dropped.

Suddenly, John understood that Bonnie was entreating him to follow her. But where to? Everything around them was alight. The roar of the fire was punctuated by the sounds of what John now realised were LPG tanks, diesel engines, farm machinery and vehicles exploding. Following her could be disastrous for both of them.

'I thought Bonnie was trying to take me back to the house. Even though I was only a few hundred metres away from home, I had no sense of direction. Everything was on fire.'

But Bonnie had never let him down before. In fact, she had proven her devotion to him time and time again. John knew without doubt that Bonnie trusted him; now she was asking him to trust her.

As he lay on the ground tangled in barbed wire, Bonnie scarpered into the bush again. And as soon as he was free, John got to his feet and followed her.

*

John plunged into the bush behind Bonnie. The smoke was so thick he worried he'd lost her, but after what seemed like an eternity, he spotted the little white dog. Bonnie was sitting patiently, almost expectantly, beside a hole. As soon as she saw John approaching she dove inside it. Without a second thought, John did the same.

'We were in this depression that was below ground level and below heat level. There was a bit of air in there, so we could breathe. It was just enough for protection,' he says.

The chaplain and his dog sheltered in that hole in the ground for four hours as the bushfire rumbled directly over their safe haven. It sounded like an earthquake, and 'felt like a bulldozer driving over the top of us'.

When they finally emerged, the landscape had been obliterated. John had sustained minor burns, and Bonnie's chest and paws were painfully singed. She was limping and shaking with shock. But they were alive.

'I didn't know that hole was there, but Bonnie just went straight to it. It's a natural instinct for an animal to look for a place to hide. I think she knew death was coming for us, and I just sort of stumbled along behind her,' he says.

Though the worst of the bushfire had passed, their ordeal was far from over. John picked his way back to the road and found his ute, now just a burnt-out shell. He made his way to the farm at the end of the road, completing the journey he had begun hours earlier. It was gone.

'All of a sudden I saw a light in the distance. I headed towards it, tripping over branches, ash in my eyes,' he says.

'It was a tractor – completely burned, but somehow one light was still going. A farmer had been trying to use it to build a fire break.'

John and Bonnie walked in the direction of the tractor owner's farm, but found most of it still ablaze. Then, as he searched a brick outhouse, 'this big hand came out and grabbed me by the throat.'

John was dragged into the toilet. 'I thought it was the grim reaper,' he laughs. In fact, it was the farmer; he had abandoned his tractor as the bushfire advanced and sought refuge in the sturdy brick dunny with his dog. The unlikely quartet sheltered there until daybreak.

'We were so dehydrated and there was no other water, so we were all drinking water out of the toilet bowl,' says John.

At first light, John ventured out onto the road, desperate to find any other signs of life. It was a decision, he says, he still regrets. He couldn't find any other people, but evidence of the fire's terrible toll was everywhere.

'I went out onto the main road and saw several cars that had had head-on collisions. I wish I hadn't looked inside them, because I saw burned bodies,' he says. 'I saw a motorbike that had melted. Everything was black.'

In the distance, he could hear the high-pitched whine of dirt bike engines. He hoped it was the CFA, Victoria's rural fire service, coming through to help at last. It made sense that bikes would be the only vehicles able to make it into the fire zone, with the roads in such a state. 'It was these people looking inside the cars, then moving on to the next one. Tears were welling up. I thought, *It's somebody coming to help me*,' he says.

It wasn't. 'As they got down to where I was, I realised they were breaking into the cars and stealing whatever they could find. Some of these cars still had deceased people in them. I heard one of them say, "Look at this poor bugger," like it was a joke.'

Even after everything he had endured in the past twenty-four hours, John says this was the worst moment. 'The amount of looting that went on afterwards was unbelievable. It just broke people's hearts. Things like that change your attitude towards humanity.'

The looters were the only people John saw for three or four days. He went home to discover that his house was now a pile of ash and twisted metal. All that had survived was an old caravan. He trekked through the bush to the home of his landlords, Owen and Jane Baylis; it was gone too. Fortunately they had made it to safety, but John later learned that Jane's parents, veteran newsreader Brian Naylor and his wife, Moiree, had perished in the blaze.

Eventually, John and Bonnie made it down the mountain to Whittlesea, where they were ushered into a Red Cross disaster relief centre. The RSPCA also had volunteers stationed in the town and they bandaged Bonnie's burned feet, which were now infected, and administered pain relief. She was obviously traumatised and shook constantly.

There were other Kinglake residents at the Red Cross centre, but John couldn't bring himself to ask about those he didn't see. It was later revealed that the Kinglake blaze had been caused by a 2-kilometre section of power lines coming down in high winds at Kilmore East, 65 kilometres north-west of the town, igniting open grassland and a pine plantation.

What John hadn't realised as he fled Kinglake was that the authorities weren't allowing anybody back in. He had lost everything in the fire, including every photograph of his beloved dog Patches. But all he wanted to do was go home – to see what was left of his home, anyway – and help. Eventually, the authorities asked John if he would be willing to go with them to search the bush around Kinglake for victims of the fire. They had heard there were recluses living in the scrub around the town and knew about John's work with marginalised people. Could he assist?

'I said yes, and we went out looking for them. We only found one caravan. We couldn't find the others because the topography had changed so much and I couldn't find my way around,' he says. 'We found one chap with his dog in his arms.'

Winter comes abruptly to Kinglake. The town was without power for three months after Black Saturday, during which time the blistering heat of summer gave way to chilly days and icy cold nights. Across Victoria's fire-hit regions, more than 7500 people had been displaced. Many of those who stayed in devastated Kinglake were now living in sheds, caravans and even tents. How could they withstand the doorhandle-deep snow that would blanket the town come July and August?

John had set up camp in his caravan, and the question of what he could do to help his community weighed heavily. He was plagued by survivor's guilt and felt that he and Bonnie hadn't yet completed their journey through the fire.

'I was thinking about what could be done to help people keep warm. There was plenty of timber. It was mostly burned, but still good underneath,' he says. 'I realised we needed a wood splitter.'

So John 'went over to the dark side' and took out the only bank loan he's ever had in his life. He used it to buy a log splitter, and for the next five winters he and Bonnie drove all over the Kinglake area splitting wood for those who needed it. The local Baptist church later paid off the loan for him and he made his deliveries in a green Mazda 121 donated by the TV production company that made the hit sitcom *Kath & Kim*. The car had been used in the show by Magda Szubanski's character, Sharon, and John soon earned the nickname 'Shaz'.

'It was an avenue I used to get into people's homes: "I'm here to split some wood for you, and by the way, how are you feeling? Is there anything else I can do for you?" There was so much need out there in the back blocks of Kinglake, but people were so embarrassed about putting their hands out,' he says. 'Bonnie has been a part of all of that. I don't think I could have done any of the work I've done without Bonnie.'

As the days after the fire stretched into weeks, months and then years, Bonnie played a special role in Kinglake's healing journey. She seemed to understand that she brought comfort to people who had lost so much, including their own pets.

'There weren't many pets left and Bonnie was one of the ones that survived. Little kids would come out to play with Bonnie. They'd throw the ball for her and she'd leg it down the street and bring it back. There was no playground any-more, but when you have a tennis ball and you have a dog, what more do you need?' says John.

'People who lost their pets would see Bonnie floating around and give her a hug. There's something about ani-mals that helps people who are hurting, people who are lonely. In her own way, Bonnie was having an impact on the healing process.'

John stayed in Kinglake for seven years after Black Saturday, but eventually he felt he had to move on. Due to his eyesight problems and the fact that he lost everything in the fire, his doctor advised him to apply for public housing. The only property available was 150 kilometres away. John took it.

'I don't think I can go back to Kinglake now. This sort of thing changes the whole concept of a little farming commu-nity that grew potatoes and carrots. That is completely gone,' he says. 'One in four people left the town, including some pioneer early-settler families.'

But while life has now taken him away from the town he called home for more than two decades, John still has his faithful Bonnie by his side.

When he was finally allowed back into Kinglake in the days after the bushfire, John went back and measured the distance from his wrecked car to that half caved-in wombat hole Bonnie had miraculously managed to sniff out. He had followed his brave, clever dog on a journey of just under half a kilometre, but it required a spiritual leap – an unshake-able belief in a little rescue dog – that few would have had the faith to make.

That's why John doesn't hesitate to use 'the M-word' to describe the journey that allowed him and Bonnie to live that day. He has no doubt that divine intervention played a part in their survival.

'Being a person of faith, I think an angel came along. It spoke to Bonnie and it led her in the direction she needed to go,' says John. 'I've raced motorcycles. I've flown aircraft. I've been in a factory fire. I've been knifed. But it was a miracle how we got out of that.'

WALKING AFTER MIDNIGHT

SISSY'S STORY

In her hit 1957 single 'Walkin' After Midnight' American singer Patsy Cline crooned about walking for miles after dark, searching for her beloved. Almost sixty years later, the classic country song could be the theme tune for another tenacious trailblazer: Sissy the miniature schnauzer. Her midnight stroll in the depths of a frigid Iowa winter made headline news all over the world – and left her owner, Nancy Franck, in no doubt about just how much Sissy loves her.

Sissy has always been the sassy one. Her brother, Barney, is sensible, protective, always checking in to make sure his sibling isn't up to no good. But Sissy likes to explore, to meet people, to cause a little bit of mischief every now and then. 'She's both naughty and nice,' says Nancy. 'She's the one who knocks over the food dish and pushes it under the counter. She's always the last one to go potty when we go out because she's too busy sniffing around.'

The dogs made their allegiances clear early on. Ever since Nancy and her husband Dale – better known as 'Bucko' – adopted the pair as eight-week-old puppies in 2004, Barney had stuck close to Nancy, while Sissy was undoubtedly 'Daddy's little girl'. But when then-64-year-old Nancy was diagnosed with cancer in late 2014 and spent almost two months away from home for treatment, both dogs were keenly aware of her absence.

After having surgery in nearby Iowa City, Nancy returned home to Cedar Rapids, a picturesque city known for its vibrant arts and cultural scene. She was admitted to Mercy Medical Center, a state-of-the-art hospital on 10th Street, just a few blocks from the banks of the Cedar River, for rehabilitation treatment. Ironically, the hospital is part of the same complex as the Hall-Perrine Cancer Center, where Nancy worked as a coder.

But her recovery was derailed when she developed a blood clot. When she started having difficulty breathing, Nancy was moved from the rehab ward to the hospital's fourth-floor Cardiac Stroke Center. She had been there for almost two weeks when, in the wee hours of Saturday, 7 February, Sissy embarked on her midnight ramble.

Twenty blocks away from the hospital, Dale was woken from a sound sleep by the insidious Iowa chill. The average overnight low temperature in Cedar Rapids in February is –7 °C and it felt every bit that frosty in the house as

66-year-old Dale realised the furnace that heats the house wasn't working.

He got the boiler firing again and then, wrapping up warm, clipped Sissy and Barney's leashes to their collars and led them out into the snow-covered yard. The leashes were a must, it was 1:30 a.m. and the Francks' garden isn't fenced; Dale wasn't about to risk the dogs dashing off into the icy night.

The call of nature duly answered, Sissy and Barney trotted back to Dale's side. He opened the front door, unclipped the dogs' leashes and they all stepped into the welcoming warmth of the house once more.

Or so Dale thought.

It was only after he'd shut the door on the biting cold that he noticed Barney was at his feet but Sissy wasn't. 'Usually I can unhook them and they'll run right back into the house. I was thinking that Sissy did, and it was cold and sometimes she'll run right into the kitchen, so I didn't think nothing about it,' Dale told Iowa Public Radio's *Talk of Iowa* show.

It was a matter of just two or three minutes, but that was all it took. When Dale opened the door again and peered out into the night, Sissy had already slipped away into the darkness.

He was frantic. He shouted her name, but his only reply was the shriek of the wind through the trees. His instinct was to charge off after her, but Dale knew that would be foolish. He wasn't in great health himself, having already spent time in the hospital that year, and had limited mobility, walking with the aid of a frame.

Instead, Dale called the local animal shelter. 'They told him to call the police department to see if they would watch for her when they were driving around,' says Nancy.

He also called one of his and Nancy's four adult children, Sarah Wood, who lives about 10 kilometres away in the town of Marion. 'I wasn't sure what to think. It was early in the morning and I wasn't awake,' Sarah told Iowa Public Radio. 'I asked him if he wanted me to come over and help look for her and he said, "No, she's got the tag on, I'm sure somebody will locate her."'

But Dale's calm demeanour hid his inner panic. 'I was scared to death,' he told *Talk of Iowa*. 'I was crying. I'm sorry, but that's my baby. My sweet puppy.'

Working the night shift on a Saturday wasn't so bad when it was so miserable out there. The wind howled and rain lashed the footpath, turning the earlier snowfall to treacherous sludge. It was just after 5 a.m., close to dawn, but with such heavy cloud cover Mercy Medical Center security officer Samantha Conrad knew there would be no warmth in the weak sunlight that day.

Samantha felt a little sorry for her colleague, who was about to leave the cosy cocoon of the security office to patrol the parking lot. She was glad she wouldn't be the one having to avoid slush puddles and slippery sidewalks.

As they chatted, Samantha suddenly saw a fleeting movement from the corner of her eye. 'I can't remember what we were talking about, but something caught my eye and I couldn't help but point and say, "Dog?" right in the middle of my sentence,' she says.

Sure enough, a small, wet, straggly dog stood expectantly in the middle of the hospital lobby. Security cameras had captured her arrival, too. She had walked into the complex via two sets of automatic doors, then turned and watched them close behind her before making her way across the foyer toward the security office.

'She had rounded the corner of the front entrance area and was looking around, ears all pointed and very attentive,' says Samantha. 'We ran out of the office and went up to the dog, who seemed very excited and a little scared at the same time.'

In her two years at Mercy, Samantha had encountered her fair share of unusual visitors to the hospital – but this was a first. 'We have had deer, raccoons and birds make their way in through the loading-dock doors, or the vestibules of our ramp entrances, but all have been contained and not in the medical portion of the hospital,' she says.

'I've also dealt with dogs running around outside the hospital, but none has ever made it as far as this one. For a dog to come into the main entrance area was a new one for the security department history books.'

The automatic doors slid open again and another early-morning visitor entered; a human this time. He hurried into the lobby, pausing to look at the dog.

'Is she yours?' Samantha asked the man. He shook his head.

The little dog was shivering with cold, her salt-and-pepper coat sodden. 'It had been raining and windy outside, so I grabbed a towel and attempted to dry her off,' she says.

That was when she noticed the dog was wearing a collar, and from it swung a tag bearing a phone number and a name: Sissy.

Samantha bundled the dog up and carried her into the security office, where she picked up the phone and dialed the number on the tag. It was Nancy Franck's home number. Dale answered.

When she told him she had Sissy, Samantha says Dale was overwhelmed. 'He talked about how Nancy was in the hospital and said that Sissy must have gotten out to find her. He explained that he had let Sissy and his other dog out to go to the restroom and must have forgotten to close the door. I assumed he meant that he was in the hospital visiting Nancy and had left Sissy in the car.'

When Dale told Samantha he was talking about the front door of his *house*, she was stunned. Spunky, determined Sassy had staged a great escape, walking more than 15 kilometres through rain, wind and snow in the dead of night. She had braved sub-zero temperatures in the canine equivalent of bare feet and a light jacket. She had crossed major city streets, busy with traffic even at that hour. And it seemed she had made her arduous journey with one goal in mind: finding Nancy.

'Dale was just as shocked as I was when we deciphered how far Sissy had travelled to make it to the hospital,' says Samantha. 'Sissy is normally the more laidback of the two dogs, so this was extremely out of character.'

Even more incredibly, Sissy had never been to the hospital before. She and Barney had been in Dale's car a couple of times when he came to collect Nancy from work at the Hall-Perrine Cancer Center, which is housed in a separate building. While it is accessible via the hospital, the dogs had never been inside.

Did Sissy know that Nancy was in the hospital, several floors above the lobby she had ambled into? And if so, *how?* Scientists believe a dog's scenting ability is a powerful weapon in its navigational arsenal. A dog that has previously walked a route can often follow the same path by tracking its own scent – but Sissy had never walked to the hospital. The scent of a dog's owner can prove equally irresistible and is easily traced in the right conditions. But in rain and snow? And when the owner is one of hundreds of people in a hospital brimming with pungent smells?

Nancy isn't sure how she managed it, but she's sure Sissy's journey was no accident. 'She was on a mission to find me. It was snowy and wet out. It wasn't a comfortable thing for her at all,' she says. 'Dale always said that Sissy was his dog and Barney was my dog, but she was the one who came to the hospital to find me.'

She even wonders if Sissy had perhaps planned her daring journey in advance, and was just waiting for a chance to put her scheme into action. 'I know dogs "talk" and I wonder if Sissy mentioned to Barney, "This is what I'm going to do."'

Amazing though her feat was, there was no getting around the fact that dogs don't belong in hospitals. Once the thrill of her arrival had calmed a little, Samantha knew that Sissy had to go.

'To be completely honest, when Sissy was first discovered my priority was to track the owner down and, so to speak, get the dog out of the hospital,' she says. 'I was extremely thankful that Dale answered the phone, because if he hadn't been able to find someone to pick her up I would have had to contact Animal Control to take her to the pound.'

Dale's own health issues meant he couldn't make the trip to collect Sissy, so he called Sarah again. When he told his daughter that Sissy was at the hospital, 'I didn't believe him at first, but it's not something you make up,' Sarah told *Talk of Iowa*.

Nonetheless, Sarah climbed into her car and began the 15-minute drive from Marion to retrieve the courageous canine.

But Sissy seemed adamant that her visit was not yet over. Her gaze seemed to be fixed on the bank of elevators in the lobby. Was she trying to figure out which one would take her to Nancy?

'After I talked to Dale, I couldn't help but notice that Sissy was parked at the front door, looking out into the hallway like she was scanning for something,' Samantha says. 'I attempted to get her attention and play with her, with no luck. I even had some crackers that I attempted to bribe her with. Nothing. I was not even a blip on her radar.'

Dale had told Samantha about his own health struggles, and about how hard Nancy was fighting to stay healthy. He was sad that his wife, who was close to retiring and excited about spending more time with her eight grandchildren and great-grandson, was facing such a tough battle.

An idea started to form in Samantha's mind. 'Both Nancy and Dale had been through a lot and all I wanted to do was help in any way I could. I am a huge dog lover, and I know I would be happy if my dog could visit me in the hospital,' she says.

Sarah's arrival soon after strengthened her resolve. 'Sissy was excited to see Sarah, but didn't seem excited when Sarah talked about taking her home!'

For her part, Sarah was shocked to find Sissy inside the hospital. She had imagined that Sissy had been spotted in the parking lot by a patrolling security officer, and expected to arrive and find her enjoying a ride-along.

'I said, "I know that this is probably not in the hospital regulations, but this is a dog that came from twenty blocks away,"' Sarah told the radio show. '"She got here in the middle of the night, and I don't know how she knew, but her mum's upstairs. Can we take her up just so Mum can see her?"'

It was precisely what Samantha had been thinking. She called the house supervisor, who is responsible for the running of the hospital after hours. Allowing animals into the wards usually required the approval of the hospital's administration, but Samantha asked the supervisor if Sissy could be permitted a brief visit with Nancy. After all, she had gone to such great lengths to get there.

The supervisor agreed, and Samantha escorted Sarah and Sissy into the elevator and up to Nancy's room. Nancy thought she was seeing things when Sarah walked in with a 'wet and wiggly' Sissy tucked under her arm.

'I accused my daughter of sneaking Sissy in but she said, "No, she snuck herself in!"' Nancy laughs. 'Sissy was wriggling, whining and squirming to see me. I think she was happy because she'd managed to do what she set out to do.'

After ten minutes, it was time to take Sissy home – she was exhausted after her unexpected adventure, and besides, Nancy knew Dale wouldn't rest until he had his girl back by his side.

But the excitement of Sissy's midnight journey lingered long after the little dog herself had left the building. 'Sissy put a lot of people in happy spirits around the hospital,' says Samantha. 'To this day I still have random people that come up to me and ask about "that dog that came into the hospital". It's wonderful to know an animal can lift so many people up and put a smile on their faces.'

*

Nancy was finally able to leave Mercy Medical Center on 8 March 2015. She had been through chemotherapy and radiotherapy, but by April her hair had started to grow back.

Sissy's road trip garnered national and international attention. The intrepid canine was featured on news bulletins as far away as England, Scotland and Japan. She even got a mention on the popular daytime cooking show, *The Rachael Ray Show*.

Sadly, more heartbreak lay ahead for Nancy. On 16 April, Dale passed away, just two weeks before his and Nancy's forty-second wedding anniversary. His death was hard on everyone, including the dogs. Sissy had always slept in Dale's bedroom – Nancy moved into her own room after Dale retired in 2008, so as not to disturb him when she got up for work – and couldn't understand where her companion had gone.

But just as she proved when Nancy was in the hospital, Sissy is every bit as devoted to Nancy as she was to Dale. She never really played favourites, much as Nancy and Dale liked to joke that she did.

'Sissy and Barney knew when Dale passed; they realised something was different, and they've been very comforting,' says Nancy. 'Several times when I've sat and cried, one has been on one side of me and one has been on the other. And Sissy comes into my bedroom at night now.'

There was one more accolade in store for Sissy. In January 2016, her devotion to Nancy was rewarded when she won the Most Amazing Journey category in the inaugural World

Dog Awards. Nancy and Sissy were flown from Cedar Rapids to Los Angeles to collect her trophy – a golden fire hydrant – at a star-studded Hollywood ceremony.

'She didn't care for it because she had to be in a carrier. At one point she got out of the bag and ran off ahead of us,' Nancy says. This time, happily, they managed to coax Sissy back before she embarked on another heroic journey. 'She was greeting everyone and seemed very happy to meet people. She likes to meet people, because she likes to be loved.'

And Sissy likes to love, too. After all, she went out walking after midnight, and walked for miles along the highway, searching for the owner she adores. Well, as Patsy Cline might have said, that's just Sissy's way of saying 'I love you'.

CARRIED AWAY

CARRY'S STORY

The 5000-odd residents of Chinchilla, 300 kilometres north-west of Brisbane in the Darling Downs, are no strangers to floods. Established on the banks of Charleys Creek in 1877, and with the Condamine River on its southern outskirts, there's water on the ground in Chinchilla once or twice a year on average. There's usually ample advance warning and plenty of opportunity for local farmers to summon their best working dogs and move the cattle, sheep and pigs that are the region's backbone to higher ground.

Dave Winfield is one of those farmers. He runs cattle on half a dozen properties across the western slopes of the Great Dividing Range, spanning some 14000 acres in total. Three of those parcels of land are located around Chinchilla, and there's another 8000 acres up near Mundubbera, nearly three hours north. Before settling in the Downs, Dave and his family – wife Jen and their two teenage sons – spent time at Beaudesert, 80 kilometres south of Brisbane and fairly flood prone itself, and in Birdsville, near the South Australian border, where flooding rains can isolate the tiny town for weeks at a time. It's safe to say Dave has seen more floods than many people have had hot dinners.

But the ferocity of the floods that swept across vast swathes of Queensland during the summer of 2010–11 took everyone by surprise, even Dave. 'We had plenty of warning that we were going to be flooded, but the water had never come up that high in recent times,' he says.

'There's a sign at the Chinchilla Weir that's eight foot high. I came across there with the State Emergency Service (SES) and we could see the water swirling on this sign. There was that much water, it was above there.'

The deluge was the most destructive in Queensland in over a century, forcing the evacuation of more than 200 000 people from ninety towns and cities, with communities along the Fitzroy and Burnett rivers hardest hit. The Condamine, Balonne and Mary rivers also burst their banks, while an unexpected flash flood inundated Toowoomba, 125 kilometres west of Brisbane, and decimated everything in its path in the Lockyer Valley.

Thousands of homes went underwater in Brisbane itself, and in Ipswich, 40 kilometres to the west, when the Brisbane River flooded. The surge pushed Brisbane's Wivenhoe Dam to almost double its normal water-supply storage capacity.

The dam has two emergency spillways designed to handle excess floodwater; one filled completely and the second peaked with just 60 centimetres to spare. More than 55 000 volunteers from all over the country registered to help clean up the city streets.

Three quarters of Queensland's council areas were declared disaster zones, and the damage bill was put at $2.38 billion. In total, this catastrophic wet summer punched a $40 billion hole in Australia's economy.

Far more devastating than the financial cost, however, was the human toll. The floods claimed thirty-five lives. Sixteen people lost their lives in the hamlets of the Lockyer Valley, including Grantham, Murphys Creek and Postmans Ridge.

The extent of the emergency rattled the entire country. As tales of tragedy, heroism, persistence and against-all-odds survival emerged, more than $11 million was raised by public disaster-relief appeals.

Domestic pets also suffered, especially in cities and towns, with dogs and cats swept away by the raging water or reluctantly left behind by heartbroken owners who had no other option. Wildlife agencies held grave fears for the native animal population too, especially small macropods like wallabies, as well as bandicoots, and native rats and mice. The true scale of the effect on wildlife will never be known, as it's believed many animals that survived the initial flood later died due to the massive loss of habitat and food sources.

Livestock fared better, largely thanks to the tireless efforts of farmers like Dave and their indefatigable working dogs. As well as managing his own cattle, Dave's work back then included contract mustering. In early January 2011, at the height of the flood emergency, he was asked by staff at the Kogan Creek Power Station, 20 kilometres south-east of Chinchilla and just a handful of kilometres from his home, to move a herd of flood-bound cattle near the $1.2 billion coal-fired facility.

The night before the muster, he walked a kilometre through the water to check on the hapless bovines.

'The water level seemed to be holding then, and it was still about the same the next day, but it hadn't dropped. The cattle were stranded on a flat in three or four foot of water. They had baby calves and it wouldn't have taken much to bring it up higher, so we thought we'd have a go at moving them the next day,' he says.

There was no way he could manage it on horseback in all that water. It would have to be a boat and dogs.

And Dave knew just the dog for the job.

When the newspapers later got wind of what had happened, they all called her Carrie, but actually, it's C-A-R-R-Y. Dave's boys named her; she's the same age as his youngest and has always been the favourite among the family's dozen working dogs.

'When you've got a lot of dogs, you end up running out of names eventually. I've had dogs named One, Two, Three and Four,' Dave laughs. 'You look for any sort of sign of what to name a dog, and when the kids were little they'd always want to pick her up. They'd say, "Carry puppy?" so that's what she became.'

When it comes to his working dogs, Dave has never been too fussed about breed. Some farmers are kelpie purists – in 2012, a two-year-old red kelpie from Tasmania was sold for $12 000 at Victoria's famed Casterton Kelpie Muster, setting a new record – but Dave will 'take anything that can do the job. You can get a good dog out of two mongrels.'

As it happens though, Carry has 'a fair chunk' of kelpie in her, and more than lives up to the breed's reputation as the hardest-working dogs on the land. She may have been a middle-aged eight years old when the floods hit that summer – working dogs don't often to see old age due to accidents, injuries and the ravages of constant wear and tear – but she was an invaluable member of the pack, prized for her calm yet forceful nature.

Carry is strong with stubborn cattle, but knows when to back off too. She's not like these lunatic dogs that will work literally until they drop, Dave says. 'She's always been a good worker, but you can't overheat Carry – you can't cook her. She knows when to take a breather. Carry's got a few more brains in her head than some dogs.'

Carry had already proven her mettle at least once before the flood: Dave accidentally ran over her in his ute when she was just a tiny pup. Fortunately, it happened on soft sand and the ute wasn't loaded. Carry emerged unscathed and hadn't missed a beat since.

That January, as Dave and two power station employees battled to push the cattle out of the floodwater and onto a dry hillock created by the power station's coal-mining activities, easygoing Carry was probably the most composed member of the team.

'There was a fair bit of water across that flat, so we swam some of the cattle out with the boat and walked others. We had a few different mobs to move. At times we were walking behind them and those baby calves just kept swimming and swimming and swimming,' Dave says. 'I'm just over six foot one, but at times the water was up to my chest. Bloody oath I was scared.'

At some stage amid the stress and chaos of the muster, Dave lost sight of Carry. He didn't know if she'd run off or been swept away in the water. All he knew was he'd brought three dogs with him, but by the time he'd finished moving the cattle and was ready to make the arduous journey home he only had two.

'I don't really know how Carry got separated or where she went. I never saw her go. When you're doing stuff like that, you're just concentrating on the cattle. It was unusual for her to take off, but we weren't in a normal situation.'

He wasn't too worried to begin with. Mustering with multiple dogs in heavily timbered country, it's not uncommon to lose one every now and then. They might remain missing in action for a few hours, or even a few days, but working dogs have a keen sense of direction and they'll invariably turn up.

But when there was no sign of Carry after two days, and with the water still not receding, Dave began to doubt the tenacious mongrel would find her way home. He'd been back out to the power station to check on the cattle each day since the muster, half expecting to find Carry waiting there. He couldn't search further afield because his property was completely cut off by the flood.

Then, on the second morning following her sudden disappearance, Dave woke up to find Carry lying on the floor of his workshop. She wagged her tail when she saw him – despite the gaping hole the size of two fists in her right side.

She was very weak and obviously in pain. Dave couldn't fathom how Carry had even made it the eight kilometres home from the power station with a gash like that – but her journey was about to get even more incredible.

Farmers rely on their working dogs. They recognise their worth and appreciate them the way a chef appreciates a great set of knives or a runner a favourite pair of shoes. They know that without them they simply wouldn't be able to get the job done.

But, generally speaking, farmers are a practical bunch. If a dog isn't pulling its weight, it's hard to justify its place in the team, just like any other employee. In rural communities, working dogs that are old, injured or no longer useful aren't likely to enjoy a long retirement in the lap of luxury. It's simply the reality of life on the land.

'A lot of working dogs don't live a long time. They're a necessity, but anyone that likes dogs grows to love them,' says Dave. 'Some fellas might have twenty or thirty dogs – it just depends on how much work you've got. You don't like getting rid of them, but how many do you keep?'

This was the question Dave wrestled with as he watched Carry lying prone on the concrete workshop floor. At first he couldn't see exactly where her injuries were, but when she couldn't struggle to her feet he knew it wasn't good.

'There was only a little bit of blood, but I could tell there was something really wrong with her. She didn't want to stand up to start with, but when she did you could hear the air whistling in and out of her right lung. I've seen some pretty bad dog injuries, but this was really nasty.'

As soon as Dave heard that whistle, he knew what he was looking at. Carry had sustained a pneumothorax, which occurs when air escapes from the lung and gets trapped in the pleural cavity – the space between the lung and the chest wall. It can happen spontaneously in dogs – usually in large, deep-chested breeds – or, as in Carry's case, as the result of trauma, such as a puncture in the chest wall.

Another of Dave's working dogs had suffered a similar injury to her chest years earlier after running into an exposed tree root in long grass. But Carry's injury wasn't caused by a tree root; those were all underwater. His gut told him she'd got into a scuffle with a kangaroo and had clearly come off second best.

'There're only two things that can cause an injury like that: a roo or a wild pig. No cow is going to do that, and Carry's not a pig dog. We see pigs all the time on the muster and she's never really looked at them,' he says.

Kangaroos, on the other hand, never back down from a fight, especially when they're cornered. With their razor-sharp claws, they can rip an animal's chest open and get in between the ribs, straight into the chest cavity.

'I've seen roos pick dogs up and smash them on the ground. When they get bailed up in floodwaters, especially if they've been swimming and they're buggered and they've pulled up for a rest, they will just stand and fight.'

Dave, as pragmatic a problem-solver as they come, didn't know what to do. He had some first aid supplies at home, and was able to bandage Carry's wound. A mate down the road who had pig-hunting dogs gave him some painkillers and antibiotics to try and stave off infection.

But after making Carry as comfortable as possible, Dave was stumped. Carry was coping somehow – but for how long?

'If I called her I could get her up and walking, but she didn't want to. She'd lie down again straight away. I could have stitched her up, but there still would have been air in her chest cavity. And she wouldn't drink, so she would've been starting to get dehydrated,' he says.

Her fighting spirit, however, remained undiminshed. 'You can flick her out of the way with your boot on the muster and she'll whimper, but I could stick my whole hand in that wound that day and she just lay on the ground and wagged her tail. She's a sook, but she's tough.'

For an entire day, Dave struggled to decide what to do for his faithful worker. Despite her stoicism, she was obviously suffering – and while he didn't want to give up on her without a fight, he didn't want to prolong her pain either. Maybe the kindest thing he could do for Carry was to end her misery.

The nearest veterinary clinic was in Chinchilla, but there was no way they could get there by road. Even the vets couldn't get in or out. Chinchilla Veterinary Service's then owner, Dr Sandi Jephcott, was flooded in at her home on the other side of town. Another vet, Dr Ryan Ayres, lived in a unit attached to the clinic and was stranded there.

When Dave described Carry's injury to Dr Jephcott over the phone, she felt she could save the dog, if only Carry could get into town for treatment. Dave's mind was made up. And so, on the second day after Carry's return, he started getting organised.

'I'd had Carry a fair while. She's a good dog and she'd been through a fair bit. I didn't want to lose her that easily,' he says. 'We weren't getting to the vet by road, so she was either going to have to get there by another means, or she was going to die.'

His first thought was to try to get Carry to Chinchilla by boat. The SES was running boats back and forth across Chinchilla Weir, eight kilometres south of the town centre, to deliver food and supplies to people isolated by the water. The weir was more than 50 kilometres away by road, but with a bit of careful driving through the flood Dave reckoned he could probably get the dog onto a dinghy and into town.

Then he had a better idea. It was crazy, but it just might work.

Queensland came to a virtual standstill when the floods hit. Roads were impassable, towns were cut off, and many were without electricity and clean drinking water. The massive Kogan Creek Power Station, however, kept right on going. Keeping the 750 megawatt station – the largest in Australia – running during the disaster was crucial; for the emergency services, access to a reliable power source was quite literally a lifeline.

But the station's employees, many of whom lived in Chinchilla, couldn't get to work. There was water as far as the eye could see in all directions – driving was simply out of the question. So the station's owner, CS Energy, chartered helicopters to fly workers the 20 kilometres or so between Chinchilla and Kogan Creek for their shifts.

Dave had met two power station employees during the fateful cattle muster five days earlier. They had exchanged phone numbers so that he could check on the welfare of the cattle he'd moved, or they could call him if any more cows wandered close to the station.

It was a long shot, but it was worth a try. Dave made the call. 'I'd got on pretty well with this fella when I met him on the muster. He looked like a bit of a knockabout bloke, so I rang and just asked him, "Can I put my dog on your chopper?"'

The odds of being granted a mercy flight weren't in Carry's favour. The chartered flights were strictly for power station staff and supplies. If the company bent the rules for one 'civilian' – and his dog – there was no telling who or what else might demand passage.

Dave's power station pal worked the night shift, and Dave had caught him at home in Chinchilla during the day. But he promised to plead Carry's case to the chopper pilot on the flight out to the station that evening. Dave resigned himself to an anxious wait; Carry was growing weaker with each passing hour and he knew that getting a spot on that helicopter was her only real chance of survival.

That night, the phone rang. The station worker had been as good as his word.

'He rang me back after he got choppered out there and said, "Yeah, have her here tomorrow morning and they'll take her into town."'

There was one condition: the pilot wanted Dave's assurance that Carry wouldn't cause any problems on the flight. A terrified, gravely ill dog in a noisy helicopter several thousand feet in the air was potentially a recipe for catastrophe.

Dave looked at his dog, struggling to breathe but still fighting to live after the best part of a week in what must have been excruciating pain. 'Yeah,' he told his mate. 'Just chuck her under your feet and she'll be no trouble.'

The next morning, he duly waded through the flood-water to the power station once more to deliver Carry to the helicopter. He watched it take off with her inside, then he went home and waited.

Carry handled the ten-minute journey from Kogan Creek to the Chinchilla Showgrounds with aplomb. Not that she was in any shape to cause a ruckus even if she'd wanted to. A mate of Dave's met the chopper at the showgrounds, then he and Carry met Sandi Jephcott, the vet.

At last, it seemed luck might be on Carry's side. Dr Jephcott lived on the dry side of Charleys Creek and, based on Dave's description of Carry's injury, thought she might be able to do something for the poor dog on the spot with equipment she'd brought from home.

It took just a glance at Carry, however, for Dr Jephcott to realise the extent of the damage. A pneumothorax wasn't something an open-air patch job at a showground was going to fix. Carry needed proper surgical treatment in a veterinary clinic, and quickly.

Unable to reach Chinchilla Vet Services by road, even though it was less than a kilometre away, Dave's mate Russell and Dr Jephcott trudged on foot with Carry through submerged agricultural plots belonging to the local high school.

At last they reached the clinic, and Carry was rushed into surgery. In a two-hour operation, Dr Ayres and vet nurse Katherine Dougall removed nearly half a litre of air from Carry's pleural cavity. Without the surgery, she would not have survived another day.

Carry being Carry, she took it all in her stride. She may have been mere hours from death, but she sailed through the surgery and recovered beautifully.

'Incredibly, she was as right as rain. She felt a million dollars,' Dr Jephcott said. 'Carry's a tough dog, but she's funny because she hates needles and having her temperature taken.'

Her return to rude health may have had something to do with her extended period of recuperation. It was weeks before the floodwater receded enough to allow Dave and his family to make the journey into town to collect their girl. Their property was flood-bound for twenty-seven days all up, and Carry was certainly lavished with love and care during that time.

When she got home, it was business as usual. Carry went back to work, and even after her ordeal remained one of the best dogs on the muster. She's thirteen now and 'still a half handy dog', according to Dave.

'She's getting on a bit now for a working dog, but she still comes out occasionally. She's an old grandma. She comes and helps when she wants to, but she also lies around a lot.'

Not that Dave minds too much. He figures Carry has earned herself a cushy retirement. 'After all the things she's been through, she's turned into a pet now,' he admits.

In the midst of the emergency, Dave didn't spend much time dwelling on the incredible journey that saved Carry's life. Not many dogs have faced down an angry kangaroo, been airlifted out of dangerous floodwater and lived to tell the tale.

But even with the benefit of hindsight, Dave isn't convinced a hard worker like Carry would have been particularly fussed about the drama.

'It was just lucky that we were moving those cattle and met those fellas from the power station, otherwise I wouldn't have been able to get her out,' he says. 'Then again, if we hadn't been down there, she might not have run off and been injured. Who knows? Plenty of things happen in the life of a working dog.'

True, but it takes a pretty special kelpie to live a life like Carry's.

RESCUING ROSIE

ROSIE'S STORY

Not all journeys are geographical. They don't always involve covering a distance between point A and point B. They might not involve travel at all. Some journeys are instead voyages of the soul. Those who make them may start out in one place and end up somewhere very different, all without ever taking a single tangible step.

Some journeys are physical, and some are spiritual. Rosie the poodle's incredible journey was both.

It was 23 October 2010, and the dazzling late spring sunshine was a little more than Alice Bennett could cope with so early in the morning. Alice and her older sister Lucy had enjoyed an evening on the town in the Tasmanian capital, Hobart, the night before, and were feeling a little delicate as they drove the 55 kilometres east to Dunalley, where Alice lived with her farmer fiancé, Tom

Gray. A busy wedding photographer, Alice had a ceremony to prepare for later on that sunny Saturday, hence the early start.

The sisters were just fifteen minutes from home on Sugarloaf Road, halfway between the hamlets of Forcett and Connellys Marsh, when they spotted a 'brown lump of fluff' at the roadside. Alice thought it was a wombat; it was about the right size and the nocturnal marsupials were common in the area. Sadly, wombats were also often struck by cars at night on the dark country roads.

But suddenly, Lucy yelled 'Stop!' and Alice hit the brakes. 'I pulled the car over and Lucy ran out and just picked this thing up,' she says.

The brown lump of fluff wasn't a wombat at all. It was a dog. A poodle to be precise, though it was difficult to tell. Its chocolate-brown fur was matted and smelly, and beneath that the dog seemed to be frail and underweight. It had obviously been a very long time since the creature had seen a decent meal, much less a grooming salon.

'We thought, *What are we going to do?*' Alice recalls. 'We decided we had to see if anybody nearby owned him, but at the same time I was thinking that whoever *did* own him didn't deserve to have him.'

Finding the dog's owner wasn't going to be as simple as strolling across manicured front lawns and knocking on doors. This wasn't a suburban street; it was the bush. Alice and Lucy were effectively in the middle of nowhere, which made the dog's presence there all the more unusual.

Eventually they did find a home, secreted at the end of a long driveway. 'We asked the man who lived there if he knew anything about the dog and he said it had been sitting beside the road for at least a couple of days. He said his son wanted to catch and keep it, but it wouldn't let him touch it,' she says.

Alice's heart sank. Could the little dog really have been waiting there all that time? Dozens, perhaps even hundreds of vehicles must have driven past the animal. How was it possible that nobody had managed – or bothered – to pick him up?

In that instant, Alice's mind was made up: the dog was coming home with her.

She and Lucy bundled the poodle into the car and continued on to Dunalley, a tiny fishing village on the road to Port Arthur. When they arrived, Lucy strode into the house with the dog in her arms. 'You're keeping him,' she announced to Tom.

Tom took one look at the down-and-out canine and said, 'It's a girl.'

Sure enough, 'he' was indeed a 'she'. After feeding her a hearty meal, Alice sat the frightened dog in the laundry tub and took a pair of scissors to her fetid fur. 'She just sat there as I trimmed all her hair back,' she says. 'She had obviously been groomed before, but not for a very, very long time. She probably had two years' worth of growth.'

The dog's ears were also clearly infected, and she seemed generally lethargic and unwell. She was weak and surprisingly quiet. Most shocking, however, was the realisation that she had recently given birth. Her engorged teats suggested that somewhere out there, a litter of puppies were being deprived of their mother's milk.

The heartbreaking discovery raised a raft of new questions. How had the dog come to be separated from her puppies? Were they still out there in the bush, exposed to the elements and in desperate need of their mother's care? It may have been sunny, but it was cool. The mercury struggled to reach the twenties in that neck of the woods in October, and at night the temperature plummeted to single digits.

Much as she wanted to stay at home and tend to the new family member, Alice had a wedding to photograph. While she went to work, Tom's mother, Penny, and Lucy drove back to Sugarloaf Road and plunged into the bush.

'They went back to where we'd found the dog thinking there must be some puppies there. They searched and searched and searched, and those puppies weren't anywhere,' Alice says. 'That made us think that someone had dumped her and kept the puppies. I just can't imagine that she walked for miles and miles in her condition. There's no question in my mind that she was brought to that spot, and was waiting there for whoever had left her to come back.'

At work, Alice couldn't stop thinking about the little dog. As she snapped pictures of the beautiful bride and groom, her mind kept wandering to that desolate roadside spot. She wondered what horrors the poodle – and possibly her puppies – had endured before she found herself alone by the highway. What would have become of her if Alice and Lucy hadn't happened upon her when they did?

The bride's mind wasn't on the task at hand either. She was upset about something, and it was obvious in the pictures. 'I thought, *I've got to cheer her up,* so I told her about this little dog I'd just found,' Alice says. 'She was so moved, and she started telling me all about how much her own dog meant to her. Her dog was called Rosie.'

The way the young woman's mood changed when she started talking about her pet reinforced for Alice just what a meaningful role dogs can play in people's lives. She may have rescued an abandoned poodle, but something told her that poodle was going to return the favour in countless ways.

In honour of the bride and her bond with her dog, Alice decided to name her unexpected new family member Rosie. Besides, a rose was a beautiful flower, and she knew that under all that fur and filth, her Rosie was beautiful, too.

The wedding photography done and dusted, the next leg of Rosie's journey was to the vet first thing Monday morning. Her ears needed medical attention, and Alice was worried that her state of neglect hid other injuries. At the same time, however, she was concerned that she could lose Rosie.

'I knew that if I took her to the vet and said she was a lost dog, by rights she'd have to go to the pound to see if anyone would claim her. I was so worried that whoever did this nasty thing to this dog would be allowed to take her back,' she explains.

So, with Lucy's help, Alice hatched a plan. They drove to the veterinary hospital and hid Rosie in the car, then persuaded a sympathetic vet nurse to sneak the clinic's portable microchip scanner outside in her lunch break.

She scanned Rosie and found no microchip. On one hand, this was disappointing: it meant that nobody was ever likely to be held to account for abusing Rosie or dumping her in the bush. But on the other hand, it was good news – it meant Rosie was officially Alice's dog.

Although it was Lucy who actually plucked Rosie from her roadside vigil, there had never been any question that the little poodle would live with Alice and Tom. 'There was never any doubt. Lucy had a dog, Lottie, and there was no way she would have let another dog into Lucy's life,' says Alice. 'Rosie was always going to be my dog.'

With her guardianship settled, Alice ventured into the clinic. Trouble was, she had told the vet nurse a tiny fib just so there was absolutely no uncertainty about Rosie's newly minted membership of the family.

'I had said, "This was my aunt's dog, but my aunt passed away and she's mine now. I want her microchipped in my name right now!"' she laughs. Once the microchip had been duly inserted, however, Alice confessed the truth about Rosie's rescue. 'I was embarrassed to think that someone would think a family member of mine would treat a dog so horrendously. The vet was very sympathetic to our cause,' she says.

The vet estimated Rosie was between three and five years old, and confirmed she had given birth to a litter of pups no more than two weeks earlier. Her ears were riddled with infection. Clinic staff also shared Alice's suspicion that Rosie had never been a beloved family pet. In fact, they guessed that given her condition and the circumstances around her roadside discovery she had either escaped from or been dumped by a puppy factory.

Puppy factories are intensive commercial breeding facilities. They supply puppies to pet shops or sell them direct to the public. According to Oscar's Law, a campaign against the puppy trade, puppy factory dogs are frequently denied adequate food, water and shelter, and their veterinary care and social needs are often completely disregarded. Breeding dogs are confined their entire lives and forced to breed back-to-back litters. Their puppies are taken to be sold at just a few weeks old. Many puppy factory dogs suffer painful, untreated health conditions including eye infections, ear infections and mammary tumours. Under current legislation, puppy farms are not illegal; the RSPCA has the power to investigate these facilities, but can only seize dogs in cases of severe cruelty or breaches of the code of practice.

But while it's certainly possible that Rosie came from a puppy factory, so-called 'puppy farmers' rarely dump their breeding animals. According to anti–puppy factory campaigners, they will breed from them for as long as possible and then kill them. It's also unusual for puppy factory dogs to escape, especially if they have recently had puppies. Campaigners have reported seeing rescued dogs fighting to get back into filthy breeding sheds in search of their pups.

In Rosie's case, the most likely scenario is that she was driven to Sugarloaf Road and abandoned there by a backyard breeder or heartless owner. But whatever her beginnings, Alice was determined that the rest of Rosie's life would be filled with the love and care she deserved. Her geographical journey had brought her from goodness-knows-where to a 175-year-old homestead on a historic sheep property that has been in the Gray family for three generations. Her spiritual journey would prove to be just as incredible.

It wasn't easy in the beginning. Two months after her rescue, a grass seed worked its way into Rosie's stomach. Stoic Rosie never let on how much pain she was in. 'We didn't see any problem until she was all swollen up and basically unconscious,' says Alice. It took two surgeries to repair the damage. Unsurprisingly, Rosie isn't allowed to walk in the paddocks in grass-seed season anymore.

But the scars of Rosie's former life went much deeper than her rancid ears and overgrown coat. She was terrified of men, and it took some time for her to bond with Tom. By the time he and Alice married four months after her rescue, however, Rosie was besotted with him.

'She adores Tom now. She even sleeps on his chest,' Alice says. 'She's the sweetest, gentlest little thing.'

She rarely barked in those early days, except for the occasional yip at a possum in the garden. Even today, the only time Rosie makes a sound is if a stranger comes to the house. This is common in neglected and abused dogs. They don't bark because they've learned there's no point; their needs will remain unmet regardless, and making noise may lead to further abuse.

Rosie also displayed extreme separation anxiety. 'She couldn't be left alone. In the beginning, if we left the house we'd leave her in our walled garden and she would try to dig her way out to the point where her little paws and face would be covered in blood,' says Alice. 'People would come to the house and see this damage to the garden and say, "What sort of pet do you have?" They'd always be surprised when we told them we had a very small poodle.'

These days, Rosie has an enormous wooden crate stationed on the back deck from where she can safely supervise the property. But she still hasn't learned to enjoy her own company. 'We live and work on our farm so she's never alone for long periods of time, but even if I'm gone for ten minutes she'll scratch and scratch against the door,' she says.

In January 2013, just over two years after her rescue, soft-hearted Rosie faced another challenge when devastating bushfires swept across south-eastern Tasmania. Dunalley was one of the hardest hit towns, with 65 properties destroyed, including the bakery, police station and primary school. Alice and Tom's entire property was ablaze, with the Gray family forced to run to the beach.

'I spent four and a half hours in the water with my baby son, James, who would turn one just three days after the fire, Lucy, Penny, Tom's aunt Deb and seven dogs, including all the working dogs from the farm,' she recalls. 'Poor Rosie has always hated getting her feet wet, so she had to be carried the whole time, and dunked under every now and then just to cool her down.'

True to form, Rosie didn't make a sound throughout the terrifying ordeal. 'We were joking and laughing, because we had James with us and that's what you do, but Rosie obviously knew something very serious was going on.'

Since that terrible day, Rosie has been more devoted to Alice than ever. 'If I go for a walk I'll be looking around thinking, *Where's Rosie?* and then I'll look down and she'll be right at my ankles,' she says. 'So close to me I don't even see her.'

Now aged somewhere between eight and ten, Rosie has transformed from a frightened, distrustful wreck into a friendly and loving – and loved – family pet. Alice tries not to dwell on what Rosie's life was like before they found each other, but sometimes she catches herself wondering where the little dog came from, and what she worked so hard to overcome. She thinks about Rosie's puppies and wonders whether Rosie thinks about them too.

'The one time I really did think about her previous life, and felt very sad about it, was when I was pregnant with

James,' Alice says. 'I think she knew that I was pregnant. She was very interested in my tummy the whole time, and when I was breastfeeding she'd be snuggled in as close as she could get, with her head on my shoulder.'

Both James and his younger brother, Barclay, share a special bond with Rosie, and their loving attention has helped bring her even further out of her shell. She has even worked up the nerve to voluntarily dip her toes in the water every now and then. 'Our farm is on the coast so we're at the beach all the time. She runs around, and if the boys are in the shallows she'll be in there splashing around with them,' she says. 'She's just happy to play with the boys.'

Alice doesn't work as a wedding photographer anymore. Together with friends and neighbours Matt and Vanessa Dunbabin, Alice and Tom now run the award-winning Bangor Wine & Oyster Shed restaurant at Dunalley. Tom farms the oysters, and the enterprise is thriving. Life is busy, especially with two boisterous young boys in the picture, but gentle Rosie keeps up with the hectic pace.

Alice says she never could have imagined how a brown lump of fluff would become such an integral part of her family, but her split-second decision to save a dog in need has been rewarded tenfold.

'I've always had dogs, but they were family dogs. There's something about finding a little dog that needs your help that is just so special,' she says. 'When we rescued her, it was like she looked at us and said, "Thank you."'

It's likely no one will ever know exactly where Rosie's physical journey began, but her spiritual journey commenced the day Alice found her beside that lonely country road. And there's no doubt about where her journey will someday end: in the loving arms of the family that rescued her.

OPERATION DESERT DOG

ILY'S STORY

To truly appreciate the astonishing story of Ily, we need to travel back in time. We must turn the clock back nearly a decade, to a point long before Ily made her incredible 69-day journey across the scorching Arizona desert. Ily's tale begins much earlier. It begins, in fact, in the days before there ever was an Ily, when there was just a Razy and a Rose.

Rose Sharman adopted Razy, a Boston terrier, in 2005 and he was her constant companion for the next eight years. He even accompanied Rose, a passionate trail runner and ultra-endurance athlete, on her regular runs of up to 40 kilometres in the foothills surrounding their home in the desert city of Phoenix.

Sadly, when he was about six, Razy contracted coccidioidomycosis, also known as Valley Fever, a fungal infection that affects both humans and dogs and is common in the south-western United States. Around 70 per cent of dogs that contract the disease display no symptoms and make a full recovery. Razy was not so lucky. The infection spread and he became gravely ill. Ultimately, both of his eyes had to be removed to save his life.

'Razy came into my life at a time when I really needed my heart taken care of, and he did a spectacular job,' says Rose. 'He was my constant companion and forever my cheering section. His little body wiggled with joy and excitement and his tongue would loll about whenever he saw me. This dog saved my heart from breaking, so when he became completely blind I knew he needed a guide dog.'

Rose adopted a female cattle dog called Heffie, and the bond between Razy and his new 'eyes' was instantaneous. 'Heffie's whole life was wrapped up in taking care of Razy. She wore a little jingle bell and I would say, "Go get Razy" and she'd find him and bring him to me,' she says.

With Heffie's help, Razy was even able to resume his beloved long runs with Rose. 'We'd still go out running on the trails and I'd say to Heffie, "Keep him on the trail!" and she'd nip his little bottom.'

As well as being Razy's sentinel, Heffie was a joyful character in her own right. Every morning, she and Rose would dance together, turning the radio up loud as they jumped, twirled and giggled their way around the house. When Razy passed away in 2012, both Rose and Heffie were devastated. His heart had never recovered from the ravages of Valley Fever, and he had developed congestive heart failure.

'He was too weak to move about the house much so I had to let him pass over the Rainbow Bridge. It physically caused pain in my soul and still does to this day that I couldn't save him,' she says.

'After Razy died, Heffie wouldn't dance anymore. She just walked around the house with her head hung. I knew she needed company, but I couldn't face getting another dog.'

Rose's deep love of animals has been a part of her for as long as she can remember. As a child, she had pet hamsters and birds, as well as a dog and a cat. Raising her family in arid, sun-baked Arizona, she grew used to the kids bringing home lizards and other creatures they'd found in the surrounding wilderness. 'They'd bring animals in and ask to keep them and I'd say, "You can't keep it in a pen, but you can keep it in the house,"' she says. 'I've always been very open to whatever nature wants to bring me.'

Her affinity with all creatures great and small extends beyond the tangible; Rose says she communicates with her pets, too. So when Razy appeared in a dream a month after he died and told her it was time to bring another dog into the family, she paid close attention.

'My dogs communicate with me; they always have. Razy came to me in a dream and said, "You're going to get another dog and you're going to name her Ily, because I love you."'

Rose felt that Razy intended the newcomer to be a cattle dog like Heffie, so she went online and visited the websites of five local dog rescue groups. On all five websites, front and centre on the homepage, was a picture of the same brown and white cattle dog. 'That just doesn't happen,' she says.

Razy was certainly making his preference known. Rose called the dog's foster carer and explained her somewhat unusual interest in the pup. 'I told her the story and said, "My late dog told me I needed to get another dog, so I need to come and see *this* dog,"' she says. 'She said, "Yes, you do – bring Heffie and come down."'

When she arrived at the carer's house, Rose sat on the floor next to the curious canine. The dog she would call Ily promptly climbed into Rose's lap, curled up and went to sleep. Then Heffie sat down beside the pair and touched her nose to Ily's. In that moment, Rose knew that Ily truly was 'a gift from Razy'.

'He and Heffie always touched each other. There was never a picture of one without the other,' she says. 'The foster carer looked at me and said, "You need to take your dog home."'

And that was that. Just as she had with Razy, Heffie immediately bonded with Ily. Heffie and Rose resumed their daily dance parties and the two dogs were soon covering up to 320 kilometres a week with Rose on her desert runs. But while Heffie preferred to relax in the shade whenever they stopped to rest or camp, Ily would immediately set off to give their surroundings the sniff test.

'Ily was always exploring to find food sources. She would come up to me with a mouthful of whatever she'd found and "ask" me if she could eat it,' Rose laughs. 'One time we were at a river and she discovered watercress. She liked it so much that she went and got a second bite and made sure Heffie had some.'

On 23 June 2013, Rose, Ily and Heffie were returning from another of their weekend adventures. They had attended the Made in the Shade Beer Tasting Festival in Flagstaff, 230 kilometres north of Phoenix, and enjoyed some stunning hiking in the surrounding mountains. Now they were heading home down Interstate 17 in Rose's luxury motorhome. At 12 metres long and weighing more than 27 000 kilograms, the enormous camper was a much-loved home away from home.

They were already on the outskirts of Phoenix when disaster struck. Just outside of Anthem, 50 kilometres from the city centre, the motorhome's front right tyre blew. Rose fought desperately to control the massive vehicle as it swerved wildly across the four-lane freeway. She managed to keep it on the road for another 500 metres, but then the road curved to the left and the wheel ploughed into the dirt of the hard shoulder. There was no way she could wrestle the behemoth back onto the bitumen.

The motorhome slammed into an embankment, obliterating the front 2 metres of it. Rose, Heffie and Ily were thrown through the windscreen and onto the road. Heffie landed 9 metres from the wreck. Rose was still buckled into her seat when it hit the asphalt, but was knocked free as it rolled repeatedly. She eventually came to rest almost

3 metres from the seat. A little further and she would have tumbled down a 20-metre cliff.

Tragically, while two-year-old Heffie had survived the crash, she died soon after. 'The first two people who arrived on the scene were an off-duty paramedic, who helped me, and a vet, and she helped Heffie pass,' says Rose.

Nobody knows where Ily landed. By the time Rose was able to ask after her, the terrified dog had vanished into the desert.

'I was a Jane Doe at that point. The contents of my purse was scattered and I didn't have any identification on me. They couldn't get into what was left of the motorhome because there was leaking fuel and propane in there,' she says. 'My recollection is that I kept saying, "There's another dog," but they thought I was confused and nobody went to look for her. I couldn't breathe; I didn't have the air to call for her, but I just remember thinking, *She's out there.*'

Rose remained conscious throughout the horrific ordeal and says she remembers 'every point of impact in detail'. She was airlifted to the John C Lincoln Medical Center in downtown Phoenix with a staggering number of injuries.

Virtually the only part of Rose's body not crushed or broken was her left arm. She had broken both legs and feet, every rib, her back and neck, her sternum and collarbone. Her pelvis was crushed and her right shoulder smashed beyond recognition. She had a fractured skull, a broken cheekbone and two of her teeth were shattered.

'From what I can tell,' Rose says, 'the only reason any of us survived is that we were athletes.'

Rose had never experienced pain like it. The agony was unrelenting, and almost unbearable. 'I'd crushed my pelvis once before and I never said I was a 10 on the pain scale then, but now I have a definition of what level 10 pain feels like,' she says. 'They couldn't ever leave me alone for the first two and a half weeks, because if I'd had the opportunity to not breathe and not be in pain, that would have been my choice.'

Rose spent two and a half weeks in intensive care, and five months in total in a hospital bed receiving round-the-clock care. But as her body slowly began to heal and the physical pain diminished, the wretched grief remained raw. Heffie's death left Rose heartbroken, but at least she was able to mourn her. Not knowing what had happened to Ily was a different kind of torment. Rose couldn't weep for the bold little girl Razy had sent her. She wouldn't, because she knew Ily had survived.

Ily had told her so.

Rose's family and friends were concerned. Her insistence that Ily was still alive was surely hindering her recovery. It just wasn't possible that Ily could have walked away from the violent crash. How could a 25-kilogram cattle dog, barely a year old, have escaped such a catastrophe with her life?

Rose knew they meant well, but she would not be swayed from her belief that Ily had made it. 'People would tell me, "You're just making this worse for yourself – she's not alive." But I said, "She is, I'm telling you, and if a time comes when she is not, I'll let you know,"' she says.

'I always knew it. I've known the moment every animal I've ever had has died. Even after the accident, when they told me Heffie was dying, I knew she was already dead. Death is when the soul leaves the body.'

Besides, Rose had insider knowledge. Heffie and Ily had warned her they would be leaving.

'One morning we were dancing and Heffie suddenly stopped. She went to the corner of the room and hung her head. I asked her what was the matter and she said, "I have to leave." I said, "What do you mean?" and she replied, "Razy needs me,"' she says. 'I looked at Ily and said, "Do you have to go, too?" She said, "Yes, but only for two or three months, and then I'll be back."'

The 'conversation' took place just ten days before the crash that claimed Heffie's life and sent Ily fleeing into the desert.

Whether or not people understood Rose's spiritual connection with her pets, plenty of others agreed that until they had proof to the contrary, it was indeed plausible that Ily could still be out there somewhere. Within hours of the accident, good Samaritans had begun to post lost-dog flyers near the crash site. As the days stretched into weeks, literally thousands of flyers were put up from Anthem all the way up to Crown King, a small mountain community 90 kilometres north.

At the same time, the troops mobilised. An unofficial search committee was established, spearheaded by Mark Happe, an acquaintance of Rose's. Volunteers working in teams of between ten and sixty people combed the desert on foot, horseback and in four-wheel-drive vehicles. They were equipped with maps and briefed on how to approach a lost dog, and even how to identify different types of animal droppings.

To this day, Rose doesn't know why so many people were so eager to help reunite her with Ily. She can only imagine the horror of the accident and the heartbreak of losing Heffie moved those who volunteered to try and give her a small glimmer of hope to cling to.

'I think 147 people took part in the search. I knew only eight of those people. People hiked hundreds of miles, covering an amazing amount of territory,' says Rose, who received constant updates in her hospital bed. 'But there were zero sightings of Ily.'

Two months passed. Though desperately worried about her little dog, Rose knew Ily wouldn't starve. Birds, lizards and nutritious grasses were plentiful, and Ily had spent much of her young life roaming the desert and knew what she could and couldn't eat. Rose also knew, however, that dehydration was an ever-present danger. Summer temperatures in the Arizona desert can soar past 48 °C, and water is scarce at best. There was also the risk of snake bite, scorpion sting or coyote attack. However she looked at it, she had to concede the odds were stacked against Ily.

But somehow Rose still knew Ily was safe. She felt it deep within her shattered bones. Their spiritual connection never faltered, even as Ily's journey grew longer and longer.

'Ily would let me "see" her every now and then. She was afraid the first day, but when she calmed down she was just enjoying the desert. She was completely happy and completely comfortable out there,' she says. 'Ily's biggest concern was that she was never going to get to run again, but I assured her I was doing everything in my power to get us better.'

Finally, as the tireless search for Ily neared its ninth week, there came a breakthrough.

'All of a sudden the team got a call and a man said, "I just saw her!" The sighting was between Anthem and the town of New River, only about six kilometres from the accident site,' she says.

The man, Jack, had spotted Ily limping across the freeway, clearly favouring one of her hind legs. He had received a flyer in his mailbox and immediately got in touch with the search team. There was a riparian zone nearby – an interface between land and a stream – so she may have been looking for water. Rescuers speculated Ily could have been attempting to return to the crash site, looking for Rose.

The next day, Ily was seen again in roughly the same spot. It was go time.

Rose was recovering at home by this time, and the rescue team wanted her to visit the area where Ily had been glimpsed. They felt that if she caught Rose's scent, Ily could be coaxed out of hiding. Rose couldn't walk. She couldn't stand, or even sit, but she was determined to do whatever it took to get her girl back.

'They loaded me into the car, a process that took over an hour. I had to lie down, but they got me out there,' she says. 'They put out a blanket and sat me on the ground for about an hour to get my scent out there.'

The rescuers had also asked Rose to bring something that only had Ily's scent on it, but this proved impossible. All of Ily's things, she realised with a pang, were Heffie's things too; they had never been apart. Instead, Rose brought a blanket infused with the scent of her daughter's dog, Sparky, who was Ily's favourite canine buddy, next to Heffie.

She knew Ily's journey was nearing its end; she just had to be patient. 'I always had in the back of my mind that she'd told me she would be gone for two to three months,' Rose recalls.

Ily didn't reveal herself that night, but the next day a third sighting was reported. Rose made the arduous and painful journey into the desert once more. 'At this point, I would do anything for her,' she says.

Everybody was hopeful, but their efforts were again in vain. If she was still out there, Ily was choosing to remain hidden in the shadows.

*

The Arizona desert may be searingly hot when the sun is up, but at 4 a.m. the cold is biting. Sherry Petta could have been tucked up in bed at home in Scottsdale, 65 kilometres away, but instead she was one of about fifteen volunteers tramping through the darkness in search of a dog she'd never seen that belonged to a woman she didn't know.

Sherry is a jazz singer with a passion for animal rescue. She runs Sherry Petta Rescue, which assists with adoptions and fundraising for rescue dogs and helps in search and rescue efforts to reunite owners with their lost pets. But she knew nothing about Rose and Ily until about six weeks after Rose's accident.

'An acquaintance who saw Rose's accident – she happened to be caught up in the traffic delay that day – had followed the story and contacted me because she knew I did this sort of thing and asked me for help,' Sherry says.

'My heart was calling me to do this because Rose had lost Heffie in the accident, and getting Ily home was the one thing that could help heal her heartache. Not to mention the fact that Ily needed us too. She'd been out there so long already and she was likely getting thinner and weaker, as well as more vulnerable to coyote attacks.'

The sightings of Ily near Anthem caused ructions among the search coordinators, who couldn't agree on how best to proceed in their quest to find her. Sherry had suggested setting a humane trap, but other searchers were dubious. Which was how she came to find herself in the desolate badlands in the middle of the night.

'We headed out into the vast desert where she'd been seen and combed the area. There were three abandoned, deteriorating dwellings where it seemed she would take cover,' she says. 'They weren't super close together, but they were close enough that she could have been hanging out at one of them, or easily moving between all three. After going out there and seeing the dwellings, I was confident that setting traps would be ideal.'

In fact, two construction workers had seen Ily near the abandoned buildings. It seemed she was using them as shade and a safe place to rest during the searing heat of the day.

After the consecutive sightings and Rose's fruitless pilgrimages out to the desert, another week passed with no trace of Ily. Sherry was worried precious time was being wasted, so she contacted a fellow rescuer, Lisa Bogart, for advice. Lisa, who is an expert at humanely trapping lost pets, suggested they contact Rose directly.

'I sent Rose a message and said all we wanted was to get Ily home . . . and we would gladly step in and get the dog. I got a call from her that same morning saying she wanted our help, so we jumped on it,' she says.

Sherry was not the only member of the search team thinking that setting a humane trap was the best option. Linda Weitzman, who had been involved from day one, had already purchased two. Sherry immediately swung into action, borrowing a third trap from a friend so the team would be able to set one up at each of the decaying dwellings. The day before the traps were set, another volunteer who had been involved in the search from the start, Natalie, had an eerie sense that Ily was nearby. She drove through the neighborhood around the decaying buildings and came face to face with the frightened dog. She watched as Ily darted into the abandoned buildings. All planned searches were cancelled and it was decided that feeding stations would be set in the buildings that night to gain Ily's trust in preparation for the actual trapping.

The team also set up baby monitors so they could listen for any sounds that suggested Ily was close by. Then, teams of volunteers sat nearby in their cars for five-hour shifts, never shifting their respective gaze from the three buildings.

Everything was riding on this.

'Ily is a very smart dog and I said to the volunteers, "You've got one shot at this. You screw this up, she's gone,"' says Rose.

It was a Sunday. The day wore on. Everyone involved was waiting with bated breath.

Nothing. Once again, clever Ily stayed well away.

The next day, Monday, Sherry and a couple of rescue friends returned to the area in the evening to post more flyers and bait the traps with warm rotisserie chicken, chosen for its mouth-watering aroma. The heat of the day was starting to dissipate and black clouds loomed.

As the sun sank below the western horizon, the wind picked up and a light rain began to fall. Arizona's monsoon season was in full swing, and the trio feared a severe thunderstorm was rolling in. They called time on the search and headed home, while the volunteers monitoring the traps hunkered down in their cars.

'I got home a little after 10 p.m. and was brushing my teeth when a call came in. It was Lynn Drewniany, one of the volunteers who was monitoring a trap that was set up in one of the dwellings,' Sherry recalls. 'She whispered to me, "I heard something. I think we got her, I think she's in the trap. I don't know what to do!"'

Smiling, Sherry replied, 'Go check!'

The moments of silence while Lynn raced out into the rain to check the trap felt like an eternity. Finally, she returned, fumbled for the phone. When she came on the line, Lynn's voice was thick with tears.

'It's her! It's her!'

It was 11:30 p.m. and Rose was on the cusp of sleep when her mobile phone trilled with a text message. She clicked it open.

It was a picture of a trap, and inside the trap was Ily.

She was frighteningly thin and looked terrified, but there was no doubt it was her girl. Ily was being transported in the trap – 'We didn't want to take any chances of Ily getting away,' says Sherry – to a 24-hour veterinary clinic not far from Rose's home. Rose's family settled her into the car, loaded her wheelchair in the back and set off to meet the cavalry.

Rose was waiting at the clinic's entrance when Lynn and her husband Curtis pulled up in the early hours of 13 August

2013 – National Dog Day. She lowered the tailgate of the SUV and Ily's liquid brown eyes peered out. Her gruelling journey was finally over. It had been nine and a half weeks since she and Rose had last seen each other.

'When she saw me through the crate she wagged her tail for the first time since she'd been in it,' Rose says.

Clinic staff carried the trap inside and set it down gently in a corridor. They didn't want to open it and risk a spooked Ily fleeing again until they had slipped a leash around her neck, but Ily was cowering in the trap and wouldn't let the vet touch her.

'I said, "If you open it and step to the side, I promise you she will come to me,"' says Rose. 'So the vet stepped aside, and as fast as she could Ily tried to climb into my lap.'

There wasn't a dry eye in the house. Word of Ily's capture had spread, and dozens of people who had been involved in the search gladly climbed out of bed and raced to the clinic to meet her.

'We all had so much love for Rose, even those of us who'd not met her before,' says Sherry. 'The thumping of Ily's tail when she first saw Rose, and how she just couldn't get close enough to Rose when she first got out of the trap, was a moving sight and a true symbol of how much dogs love their people. It was beautiful.'

Linda Weitzman, who had spent countless hours posting flyers and talking to people in the community to ensure as many as possible were aware of Ily's plight, strode over to one of the flyers she had pinned up in the clinic weeks before.

She took it down and in its place posted a flyer with 'Lost Dog' crossed out and 'FOUND' scrawled in big, bold letters under Ily's picture.

Rose turned to Sherry and the other volunteers and smiled. 'Boy,' she said, 'you girls work fast.'

But Sherry refuses to accept credit for Rose and Ily's reunion. The search was a mammoth team effort. Rose says she will be eternally indebted to all the volunteers, especially core team members Mark Happe, Maia, Curtis, Tammy, Natalie, RuthAnne and Linda.

Ultimately, Sherry has no doubt it was Rose and Ily's devotion to each other that brought Ily home.

'Rose has been an incredible inspiration to all. With the injuries she suffered, and not being able to look for herself, she had the grace to let others help,' she says. 'And since then, she has responded to others who have needed help.'

Months later, Rose joined Sherry in searching for a tiny, 4-kilogram poodle lost in the desert. Soon after Rose arrived, the little dog was found safe. 'A little part of me thinks Rose brought a little magic to that morning,' says Sherry.

Rose also bought two humane traps and donated them to the rescuers for future search efforts; it was her way of saying thank you.

In an amazing twist, Ily was found in the company of another stray dog, a pit bull mix called Buddy. He had been missing only a week, after escaping from a family that had adopted him from his original owner, a woman who had been reluctant to rehome him but felt she had no choice. Buddy's new family no longer wanted him, but his first owner gladly took him back.

Ily may have lost Heffie, but she had honoured her best friend's memory by helping another dog in need.

Ily was dehydrated and starving. She had lost more than 10 kilograms during her desert ordeal. Her left hip had been broken in the crash, and healed incorrectly in the weeks that followed, causing nerve damage. She later had surgery to repair it, but it still causes her pain and she walks with a limp.

None of her injuries, however, could dull the pure, unadulterated joy of Ily's return home.

'When she first came home she ran through the door and cried that happy, yippy cry that dogs have. She ran upstairs and downstairs, through the doggy door and out into the yard. She was just ecstatic,' says Rose.

Ily had always slept on Rose's bed, but now that her mistress was in a modified hospital bed, that wasn't possible. Instead, she set up a crate on the floor next to the bed. Ily climbed in and went straight to sleep.

'About every ten minutes I would roll over and look at her, and she'd be looking at me as if to say, "We made it, Mum."'

Rose had another surprise for Ily. About two weeks before she was found, and feeling her return was imminent, Rose started to worry that Ily would struggle without her soulmate, Heffie. So she adopted Wyatt, a 30-kilogram cattle dog-malamute mix.

'She liked Wyatt right away, but she was so frail she didn't want to interact with him or my daughter's dog, Sparky. She was weak and hungry, and they were big and healthy and wanted to roughhouse, and she did not,' she says.

In fact, Ily didn't want to do much at all for the first few days. She wouldn't leave the house, wouldn't even greet visitors at the front door. And she missed Heffie desperately.

'One day I saw Heffie. She just came and sat in the corner. Ily saw her too, and ran to the corner and cried,' Rose says. 'That was the last time she showed herself to me. I think she doesn't want to hurt Ily.'

The story of Ily's desert odyssey spread across the US and around the world as far as the UK, Australia and even Tanzania. While the tenacious canine remains unfazed by her newfound celebrity, Rose says seeing the way Ily's story has touched others has been an important part of her healing process.

'It has helped my heart immensely to see that,' she says. 'Ily's strength of character is pretty amazing.'

Rose returned to work as a dental hygienist in September 2015, more than two years after the accident. She has had more than fifteen surgeries since that terrible day; her body is now held together with 2 kilograms of metal screws and plates. She has five hours of physical therapy, three days a week.

But her progress continues to defy doctors' expectations, even if she personally finds the healing process frustratingly slow. She has even been able to resume running and hiking, covering up to 25 kilometres at a time – with Ily and Wyatt by her side, naturally.

'I wanted to get back to running because I love it, but I had another reason, and that is that Ily loves running,' she says. 'I have to do this for her.'

Slowly, Ily's innate joyfulness has crept back. She's a little more cautious these days, especially around boisterous dogs, because like Rose she lives with constant pain. But also just like Rose, Ily is on a mission to wring every last drop of happiness out of her life.

'I wake up every morning and I have a choice to be happy or not happy, and I choose happy,' she says. 'I know that every experience has a silver lining. The people I've met through this experience are incredible. I refuse to not be happy.'

Ily feels the same way. Rose knows, because Ily told her so.

FROM THAILAND WITH LOVE

RAMA'S STORY

They had waited so long for this holiday. It was November 1998, and this idyllic week lounging on the beach in Phuket, an island in Thailand's south, followed by a week in the bustling capital, Bangkok, would be a much-needed respite from Kim Fox and Gary Cooling's busy lives back home in Woodford, north-east London. Kim worked long hours as a social worker for the local council, while Gary's job as a roofer was backbreaking. All they wanted to do was eat, sleep and relax, and Thailand seemed the perfect place to do just that.

As the couple wandered through the night market in teeming Patong, drinking in the warm, fragrant air, Kim could feel her stress starting to melt away.

Then she saw the dog, and in an instant, her life changed forever.

At first glance, there was nothing particularly special about the dog weaving its way through the market patrons, sniffing for food and trying to dodge the firecrackers being thrown by some young boys. The honey-coloured creature was a stray, a 'soi dog'; *soi* is the Thai word for side-street, lane or alley. Street dogs are a common sight across the country. According to the *Bangkok Post*, there are more than 300 000 in the capital alone, and many hundreds of thousands more in Thailand's other major cities, islands and beach resorts.

But something about this emaciated animal stirred Kim's soul. She couldn't have been more than two years old and Kim could see that, despite her poor condition, she was beautiful. 'She was a "yellow dog" – a common Thai breed – but she was very distinctive. She looked like she had eyeliner around her eyes,' she recalls.

A dog lover all her life, she had long made a habit of feeding strays whenever she got the chance. She had a tin of pilchards in tomato sauce in her bag for precisely that purpose, and she offered it to the hungry canine. The dog wagged her tail and practically inhaled the fish.

'We moved on and didn't think any more of it,' says Kim. 'But she followed us.'

Kim figured she would give up and drift away once she realised there wasn't any more food on offer, but she didn't. Their hotel's taxi was waiting across a busy road thronged with speeding cars, motorcycles and *tuk-tuks*, and as Kim and Gary walked towards it, the dog was hot on their heels.

'We crossed a busy road and she was still by our side. We thought then that it would be safer for her if we took her back to the beach where our hotel was. At least then we'd be able to continue to feed her for a few days,' she says.

They bundled the dog into the taxi, where she was promptly sick. 'She brought up all the pilchards, and the driver went mad and charged us a lot of money,' says Kim, who later learned that street dogs are notoriously bad travellers.

Eventually they made it back to their beachfront hotel and spent the rest of the evening sitting on the sand with the dog. If they were going to care for her during their time in Phuket, Kim and Gary decided, she would need a name. They dubbed her 'Rama', after the Hindu god. Thai kings are also commonly referred to as Rama.

When it came time for the couple to head inside to bed, Rama shimmied under a deck chair and settled in for the night. She was still there the next morning, snoozing exactly where they had left her.

For the next week, Rama stuck like glue to Kim and Gary. She would be waiting at the hotel entrance every morning, her tail wagging, and then would accompany the couple as they explored Phuket during the day. She even dined with them in restaurants, sitting under the table waiting for tidbits.

But when Kim and Gary returned to their hotel each night, Rama would become distraught. They had to devise a strategy: Gary would go in first while Kim would distract

Rama with food and pats, then try to make a discreet exit. It rarely worked; Rama was too smart for that.

'She would run into the reception area looking for us. We'd hear a commotion and see the hotel staff running around shoving her out, trying to hit her with a broom. It broke out hearts,' she says.

Aside from the nightly drama, their week in Phuket was just the blissful holiday they had hoped for; Kim and Gary even got engaged. But as their departure to Bangkok drew nearer, the reality that they would soon have to leave Rama to an uncertain fate loomed over the happy trio like a black cloud.

'Once we spent that week with her she really got under our skin. We got very attached to her during those days. We formed a really close bond,' Kim says. 'Once she found us, she didn't want to let us go because we'd shown her some kindness and she may not have had that before. She was a very intelligent, lovely and faithful dog.'

Thai street dogs rarely live long lives. They tend to die of starvation or disease, or they become traffic casualties. The thought of something so awful happening to Rama was devastating, but there didn't seem to be much the couple could do to prevent it. They had searched for an animal shelter or street dog rescue group, but none existed in Phuket at that time. As Kim prepared to leave, she tried to console herself with the knowledge that, whatever lay ahead for Rama, at least she had known love and care for a short time.

But then Kim and Gary learned some horrifying new information. Though Phuket is a popular holiday destination all year round, November is still the low season; the majority of visitors come between December and March, when it is cooler and drier. In those days, locals told the couple, the government 'cleaned up' the island before the peak tourist season began by rounding up the street dogs and poisoning them with strychnine.

It was an abhorrent destiny, and not one Kim was prepared to accept for Rama. She didn't know how, but she was going to take Rama home to the UK – and to safety.

'I think Gary threatened to leave me once I said, "Why don't we take her back with us?" but I'd made a commitment to her,' she says. 'At the end of the day we both wanted this dog to survive, and the only way she was going to do that was if we took her with us. The idea of having her home safe with us became quite overwhelming.'

With Gary on board, the rest of the couple's time in Phuket became a whirlwind of trying to figure out how to transport a Thai street dog the 10 000 kilometres back to London.

'Spotting Rama basically ruined our holiday, because every day after we learned she was going to be poisoned was spent trying to organise her papers and her flight back to the UK,' Kim laughs.

But once the decision was made, Kim and Gary's resolve never wavered. 'The thought of leaving her to that fate was just too much. We didn't have a lot of money, but to me, to be able to buy Rama years she may not otherwise have had was just an amazing thing.'

The wheels were in motion. Rama's incredible journey had begun.

Before they could take her back to England, Kim and Gary first had to get Rama to Bangkok. After much wrangling – nobody the couple appealed to for assistance could believe they were going to so much trouble for a mangy street dog – they bought a transport crate and travelled with her on an internal flight to the Thai capital.

'When we arrived at Bangkok Airport we were going around asking, "Where's the animal reception area? Where do we collect her?"' Kim recalls. 'Then we heard someone say, "It's a dog!" and there was Rama on the baggage carousel, going around in her crate, looking quite unfazed.'

They were booked into an upmarket hotel in the city, and pleaded with the manager to allow Rama to stay in their room with them. He refused, but reluctantly allowed her to stay in her crate in the hotel's basement, where Kim and Gary could visit her whenever they liked.

Sprawling Bangkok is known for its ornate shrines and vibrant street life – but the couple didn't see much of that during their week there. Sightseeing was forgotten in favour of trying to arrange the next leg of Rama's journey to her new home. First Kim had to find a veterinary hospital that could certify her fit to travel to the UK – and one that wouldn't baulk at treating an animal many Thais regarded as being worthless.

She finally found a suitable clinic, and the vets there confirmed that Rama was about two years old. They also diagnosed her with heartworm, a parasitic roundworm that is spread by mosquitoes and most commonly infects dogs. The worms live in the heart, lungs and surrounding veins and tissues. Left untreated, the infection is fatal, with dogs usually dying from congestive heart failure.

Even the treatment for heartworm is fraught with danger: the worms and their larvae are killed with medication containing arsenic. The risks are higher for dogs with reduced heart, liver or kidney function, and Kim had no idea what condition Rama's body was in after two years of malnutrition and neglect. It wasn't possible to gauge exactly how advanced Rama's infection was either. After treatment, the vets warned she would need complete rest for several weeks to give her body time to absorb the dead worms. Any exertion or stress could cause the dead worms to break loose and travel to Rama's lungs, possibly causing fatal respiratory failure. Considering Rama – who couldn't even manage a short taxi ride without vomiting – had a potentially stressful twelve-hour flight ahead of her, this was a huge worry for Kim. Could her new dog cope with the travel?

Also a concern was the fact that few vets in the UK are familiar with heartworm. Originating in the southern United States, the parasite is now found in much of the world – but not England.

'The vets in Bangkok said the vets in the UK wouldn't know how to treat her and we wouldn't be able to get the drugs there, so we'd have to take them with us from Thailand,' Kim says. She duly purchased the drugs, which cost more than £1000. 'They also said there was a risk to her going in the plane, but because she was so young we just had to hope the infection wasn't too advanced.'

With a heartworm treatment plan in place, the next challenge was booking a place for Rama in a London quarantine facility, where she was required to stay for six months after her arrival in the UK.

Then Kim tried to book Rama onto their flight home, only to discover the crate in which she'd travelled from Phuket to Bangkok was not acceptable for an international flight.

At long last, after an incredibly trying week, everything seemed to be in order. Kim and Gary took Rama to the airport, more than ready to take their girl home. 'The whole trip to Thailand, from the minute we saw her, we were stressed,' Kim says.

And the anxiety didn't stop there. 'All the men at the airport were in hysterics, thinking it was hilarious that we were taking this dog back. We said, "Don't forget to load her," and they were all howling with laughter,' she says. 'We were worried we'd leave the country and Rama would still be sitting on the tarmac thinking *What's going on?*'

There was one more heart-stopping moment as the couple boarded the plane. 'When we were going through we said, "The dog's onboard, isn't she?" and the cabin crew said, "What dog?" Everyone on the plane saw us peering out the window and thought we were mad.'

But as they took their seats, they saw Rama's crate being loaded onto the plane. The ground staff had kindly put ice on top of the container to keep her cool in the searing Thai heat. 'We didn't relax until we saw her going up the conveyor belt into the hold and saw her beady eyes peeping out,' she says.

The moment the plane touched down at London's Heathrow Airport twelve hours later, the angst set in again. Had Rama survived the flight?

'The animal reception vehicle came out and got her off the plane before anybody else. We saw her going down the luggage belt, peering out, while we were still on the plane and we thought, *She's made it!* We were really pleased, but also really drained from it all.'

There was no time to rest, however. Kim and Gary raced home to Woodford to deposit their bags, then drove back to Heathrow to visit Rama in quarantine. Happily, 'she was absolutely fine. She seemed in great spirits.'

After the excitement – and exhaustion – of the relaxing holiday that ultimately contained no relaxation, Kim and Gary went straight back to work. Every weekend, they made the 80 kilometre, hour-long journey to the quarantine facility to see Rama.

Kim had been worried about how a Thai street dog, who was accustomed to having the freedom to roam the back-streets and beaches of Phuket at will, would cope in the kennel environment, but Rama handled it better than many of the more pampered pets there. For the first time, she had a bed, a blanket and plentiful, nutritious food. To her, it was a five-star hotel.

'She must have thought regular meals were better than being on the streets and being hungry all the time, and not knowing when someone's going to kick you,' says Kim.

The heartworm treatment was also starting to take effect, and Kim and Gary saw a remarkable change in Rama. 'We noticed how lively she was a couple of weeks later. She had been very, very lethargic at first because of the heartworm – not like a two year old dog at all – but she began to act like a puppy.'

Kim and Gary married in June 1999, soon after receiving their most important wedding gift: Rama was allowed to come home. All in all, Rama's journey from the streets of Phuket to suburban London had taken half a year and cost more than £5000.

'The day we actually went to collect her from quarantine was the happiest day of our lives. It was just a wonderful day. After that journey from Thailand, she was finally safe. She was part of the family,' says Kim. 'Rama really blossomed from that day. She knew she was with us, and she knew she was safe.'

She may have had an unorthodox journey from street dog to beloved pet, but Rama wasted no time settling into life at home with the Coolings. She quickly established herself as leader of Kim and Gary's pack of rescue dogs – they already had four canine companions adopted from UK shelters – and adored her off-leash time in nearby Epping Forest.

'She would just run and run and run. She used to chase the foxes – being a dog from Phuket, she hadn't seen them before – and climb trees and all sorts,' Kim says. 'In the winter it snowed so we got her a nice coat. She used to go out in it on tiptoe, like, "My God, this is a bit cold!"'

But while she was a remarkably well-adjusted pet given her rocky start in life, Rama hadn't escaped her old existence entirely unscathed. She abhorred rain and refused to go out in it. Her aversion to the wet stuff made sense; a street dog seeking shelter from one of Phuket's monsoonal downpours in a restaurant or shop would not have been treated kindly. She also had a lifelong phobia of having her nails clipped, and had to be anaesthetised by the vet every time the minor chore needed to be done.

In the early days of her new life in London, Rama also had severe separation anxiety. 'She hated to be apart from us. When we left her during the day she didn't think we were going to come back and she chewed up a lot of shoes and our record collection,' says Kim. 'Then suddenly she just calmed down. I think she realised that we would always come back.'

But while her anxiety eased, Rama's devotion to the woman who saved her from an unimaginable fate only strengthened. 'She was so close to me. If we ever had strangers in the house, Rama would be there in front of me keeping an eye out. She would have taken a bullet for me.'

Being part of Rama's journey inspired Kim and Gary to rescue more dogs from overseas. Over the next decade, they adopted several more Thai street dogs, as well as some strays from Sri Lanka.

Given her robust health and zest for life, Kim imagined Rama would live to a ripe old age. Sadly, it was not to be.

In early 2009, almost exactly a decade after she came home to Woodford, Kim noticed a cluster of lumps around Rama's neck. She had surgery and the lumps were successfully removed, but in April Kim found another, larger lump on Rama's shoulder. It was also removed, and a biopsy revealed lymphoma, a blood cancer that develops from lymphatic cells.

More lumps appeared. Rama had chemotherapy, and at one stage they disappeared, only to return within days, larger than ever. The cancer was taking over, and Rama was becoming sicker and sicker.

'It just overwhelmed her,' Kim says. 'She made it to about twelve, which is a good age, but we were hoping she'd get on a bit because apart from the heartworm she'd never been ill.'

On 8 June 2009, Kim and Gary made the heartbreaking decision to release Rama from her pain. As they prepared for the sad journey to the vet, Kim says Rama turned around at the doorway and gazed back at her canine friends.

'It was as if she was saying, "I'm going and I'm not coming back,"' says Kim, who held Rama in her arms as she passed away.

When the couple got home and their other dogs saw that Rama wasn't with them, they all howled. Kim and Gary did, too.

But as devastating as Rama's loss was, it wasn't the end. Her journey continued.

After Rama died, as Kim reflected on her extraordinary life and what the gentle stray had meant to her, she felt gripped by a need to do something to help other dogs like her.

'There were other dogs on that beach in Phuket and we knew they were going to be poisoned. They deserved more than that,' she says. 'It was living with Rama and thinking about those other dogs that inspired me.'

The more she thought about the street dogs, and the more she weighed Rama's gentle, loving nature against the cruelty and abuse the strays endured, the angrier she became. Kim feels that as a species humans consistently fail and betray dogs.

'We domesticate dogs and then we leave them to die on the streets without any food or water. Anything under the sun can happen to them,' she says. 'There's so much animal suffering in this world. You can only do so much as an individual, and for me it was never enough. There were never any happy endings because there was nowhere for these dogs to be safe and cared for.'

Even before Rama died, Kim had set the wheels in motion to launch her own dog rescue charity. She registered Animal SOS Sri Lanka in the UK in 2007, and set about raising money to buy a four-acre parcel of land at Galle on Sri Lanka's south-western tip. The land is now a sanctuary, which opened in June 2009 – not long after Rama's death. It is home to 780 dogs – all of whom roam freely, there are no cages – and 70 cats housed in a separate cattery. The animals will live out their days there unless they are adopted by loving families.

'We basically bought jungle. There was no electricity, no water. We dug wells. We got a building up,' says Kim, who runs the charity from the UK and visits Sri Lanka twice a year. 'We endeavour to rehome as many rehabilitated dogs and cats as possible, but finding loving forever homes is not that easy. Many dogs are kept as guard dogs in Sri Lanka, not family pets, so they end up being chained or kennelled for much of their lives. We do find good homes for a few, but sadly not enough. Most of the animals stay at the sanctuary for life, so it's a struggle.'

They even keep disabled and paralysed dogs that are unlikely to ever find new homes, equipping them with wheeled carts to give them mobility. 'We call them The Cart Gang and they're a force to be reckoned with,' she laughs. 'They're just so happy to be alive.'

As part of its community outreach programs, Animal SOS Sri Lanka also neuters, spays, administers free rabies

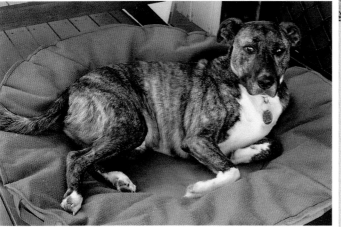

ABOVE: Handsome Occy's incredible journey amazed everyone.

LEFT: Occy was understandably exhausted after his 170km journey from Newcastle to Sydney.

ABOVE: I do! Oscar and Joanne 'married' in a Las Vegas wedding chapel, with an Elvis Presley impersonator officiating the ceremony.

BELOW: Oscar's time in China was fraught with challenges, but the opportunity to visit the Great Wall was too tempting to pass up. *Photos: Joanne Lefson, www.oscarsarc.org*

ABOVE: In every country he visited, gentle Oscar captured hearts.

BELOW: Determined to honour Oscar's memory, Joanne decided to complete their planned trip to Mount Everest Base Camp. And what better travel companion than Rupee, the dog she recued from an Indian rubbish dump?
Photos: Joanne Lefson, www.oscarsarc.org

ABOVE: John Laffan saved Bonnie from unimaginable cruelty – and she returned the favour more than once. *Photo: Captain Bronwyn Williams, Salvation Army*

ABOVE AND LEFT: Despite a troubled start in life, Rosie has grown into a calm, loving dog – and a treasured member of the Gray family.

ABOVE: BJ says he feels more connected to his pets than ever after devoted Tillie's week-long vigil for her best friend, Phoebe.

ABOVE: Ily required surgery to repair her leg, which was broken in the crash and healed incorrectly.

BELOW: Today, Ily is as energetic as ever and still loves to get out on the trails to run with her canine companion, Wyatt.

ABOVE: Never taking it off – Ludivine is understandably proud of her half marathon finisher's medal.

LEFT: Lucky was a 'foster fail'. Michele planned to care for her temporarily and then find her a loving forever home, but couldn't bring herself to part with the beautiful dog.

ABOVE: Despite a decade-long absence, Inka wasted no time making herself at home with Peter and Janneke on the Gold Coast.

LEFT: Sissy and Barney. Sissy's feat earned her the 'Most Amazing Journey' prize at the World Dog Awards.

ABOVE: Pero's incredible journey made headlines world wide, with Alan and Shan inundated with interview requests.

ABOVE: Chris Jones believes Jay chased a feral cat into this stormwater pipe and couldn't find her way out again.

BELOW: Chris and his beloved dog, Jay, have been inseparable for more than a decade.

ABOVE: Enthusiastic, energetic Bella was calm, patient Lucky's polar opposite.

ABOVE AND LEFT: When he finally made it to his forever home, Chopper was renamed Fergus. The Panzera family thinks his new name suits him much better.

ABOVE: Penny has been Colt Brown's constant companion from day one.

LEFT: An overjoyed Kendra and Colt Brown collect Penny from the airport after her unexpected adventure.

ABOVE: It didn't take long for Rama to gain weight, get healthy and fall in love with her new life in the UK.

ABOVE: Jamila wasn't convinced at first that she and Dinah were a match made in heaven, but when the little dog twice saved her life she knew they would be together forever.

vaccines and provides emergency veterinary care for sick, injured and stray animals, mostly dogs. They also treat for mange, ear infections and eye infections, which are common in street dogs. The education programs are vital, Kim says, because stray animals are often demonised due to the threat and fear of rabies. There are some cruelty cases, such as dogs having boiling water poured over them to keep them away. Unwanted puppies and kittens are frequently thrown over the sanctuary walls, which puts further pressure on the charity's already-stretched resources.

'We've had dogs that have been really aggressive because they've had really terrible experiences with people kicking them or throwing stones. These dogs can be rehabilitated if you give them time and give them a chance. Love wins the day,' she says.

'My heart goes out to the street dogs because they're on their own. Most of them have never experienced love, but they're so grateful to be rescued. Many dogs come into the sanctuary close to death, but they soon muster all their strength to wag their tails, even the ones that don't make it. They know that for once in their lives they're getting help; someone has cared enough to save them and they are so grateful for that.'

Kim has never drawn a salary from the charity, preferring as much of the money raised as possible to go to the running of the sanctuary and paying staff in Sri Lanka. The team there includes vets, vet nurses, caretakers and even cooks. They feed more than 900 animals every day – including street dogs as well as those housed at the sanctuary – and prepare more than 250 kilograms of food daily. It costs about £15 000 per month to feed and house the animals, and keep the organisation running.

For the first couple of years, Kim ran Animal SOS Sri Lanka while continuing to work full-time as a social worker, but soon realised something had to give.

'I was having to come home late, cook, do the rounds of dog walks, then get on the computer about 9 p.m. and work on charity business until the small hours of the morning,' she says. 'I ended up getting only two or three hours of sleep a night. It started affecting my health and I couldn't concentrate at work. I thought, *I can't continue like this*, but I didn't want to give up because I'd come too far.'

She took voluntary redundancy from her job to manage Animal SOS Sri Lanka full time. 'I gave up my career to make this work, but it's a labour of love for the street animals. Dogs have been the love of my life. They've given me so much. All I can do is try to give back.'

The abiding canine love of her life, of course, is Rama. She is never far from Kim's thoughts, especially on the tough days – which, in the world of running a small charity, are numerous.

Whenever a new dog arrives at the Animal SOS Sri Lanka sanctuary, the first order of business is always giving it a name. When a dog has a name, he is no longer just a 'thing'. He is a life, a soul, a being worthy of love and care. It was this philosophy that led Kim to name a little Thai street dog after a powerful god, and that decision sparked a journey that profoundly changed both of their lives. Kim and Gary's dream Thai holiday may have been ruined, but it delivered a happy ending they could never have imagined.

'I have a deep love for dogs, and I'll continue to love them. Rama inspired me. This is Rama's legacy,' Kim says. 'People often ask me, "Why does the sanctuary mean so much to you?" It's because there's a happy ending.'

THE GREAT CHOPPER CHASE

FERGUS'S STORY

It was supposed to be a new beginning; a fresh start for both a neglected, abandoned dog and a family still grieving the loss of their beloved pet. Instead, it was an impromptu journey that sparked 'an eleven-day nightmare' and ultimately proved that you don't have to know someone a long time to know you'd do anything for them.

The Panzera family is a dog-loving clan. Growing up in her native Ireland, mum Romy was a frequent adopter from the local dog shelter. Two dogs in particular shared a penchant for adventure: the intrepid pair once managed to board a bus headed for downtown Dublin, returning of their own accord hours later.

Later, when Romy moved to Melbourne and married her Italian-Australian husband, Dominic, the couple adopted two-year-old Arthur, a Rhodesian ridgeback–labrador cross who had been abused and 'was terrified of everyone and everything,' she says. He was 12 kilograms underweight, was fearful of men and very aggressive towards other dogs. It took three years of patience, love and gentle training for Arthur to blossom.

'We did a lot of work with him and he became the most beautiful dog you could wish for. It was like one day something literally switched and he went, *Life's okay*,' says Romy.

The timing was fortunate, because by that time Romy and Dominic had welcomed a son, Valentino. Over the next nine years, Arthur cemented his reputation as a model family dog, although his ongoing antipathy toward other canines meant he was never allowed off leash in public, and the children – Valentino, younger brother Rocco and baby sister Aoife – were never able to walk him.

Sadly, Arthur passed away in early 2015. 'We think he had a brain tumour, because he started having fits. One day I came home and he couldn't get up. We were all there when he died, and it was terribly sad.'

Arthur's loss hit the family from Glen Iris in Melbourne's eastern suburbs hard. After twelve wonderful years, they felt bereft without a canine companion. Coming home every day to an empty house was awful, says Romy, and it wasn't long before they felt ready to consider welcoming another four-legged family member into the fold.

Their first port of call was North Melbourne's Lort Smith Animal Hospital. The largest not-for-profit animal hospital in Australia, Lort Smith has cared for more than five million animals and rehomed some 200 000 pets since it opened its doors in 1936. When Romy clicked onto the hospital's website while at work on a frigid winter Thursday in August 2015, it was purely for research purposes. She only wanted to find out the opening hours for the adoption centre; she wasn't actually looking to get a dog right away.

But as so often happens when it comes to choosing – or being chosen by – a pet, fate had other ideas.

On the website's front page was an image of a big, black and white hound with an infectious doggy grin. 'I just fell in love,' Romy recalls. 'I rang Lort Smith immediately and said, "Tell me about this dog."'

The dog that had so beguiled her was called Chopper. He was an Irish wolfhound–Bull Arab cross who tipped the scales at a hefty 46 kilograms, despite being just eighteen months old – effectively still a puppy. Chopper had been at the shelter for six days and was, according to staff, very timid and nervous. Perhaps unsurprisingly given his size and shyness, he hadn't had a single enquiry.

To Romy, he was perfect. 'I like big dogs and, being Irish, I'm a sucker for an Irish wolfhound. Chopper's picture was funny, the way his paws were slightly splayed. And he just had this look on his face – he was like a small dog in a big dog's body.'

Shelter staff told Romy the dog seemed anxious, but assured her he wasn't dog aggressive. After managing Arthur's aggression issues for more than a decade, that was all she needed to hear. She called Dominic and suggested they take the children to meet Chopper at the weekend.

Sensing her excitement, Dominic instead suggested Romy meet him and the kids at Lort Smith after school that very day. 'I was working in the city so I scooched over there by tram. I remember thinking on the way that if this dog panicked with me or the kids there'd be an issue, but if he was okay then I definitely wanted him,' she says.

When she arrived at Lort Smith, Dominic and the children were visiting some of the other dogs that called the shelter home, so Romy went to meet Chopper alone. First impressions weren't promising. 'Chopper was this trembling, nervous, terrified creature, and I did think, *Gosh, is he too nervous for a family with three boisterous kids and a lot going on?*'

The shelter environment often makes dogs anxious and fearful; even the most outgoing hound can become distressed in unfamiliar, noisy surroundings, especially when he suddenly finds himself there after years with the same owner. Wanting to give Chopper the benefit of the doubt, the Panzeras took him outside for a short walk. Instantly, the oversized pup relaxed.

'He walked beautifully and kept checking that everyone was there, even the kids,' Romy recalls. She had loved her evening walks with Arthur, but stopped these when he became ill as she didn't feel safe walking alone. Suddenly, she could see herself walking in the dusky twilight with

Chopper by her side. 'That was it,' she says. 'Decision made.'

Romy turned to Serena Horg, general manager of Lort Smith's adoption centre, and told her the family wanted to adopt Chopper right away. From a casual visit to the website hours before, they were now going home with a new furry friend.

Serena was thrilled. In less than a week, Chopper became a firm favourite. He'd had a rough start in life. As far as Lort Smith staff could work out, his owner simply didn't have time for the dog he'd had since he was a tiny puppy.

'Chopper was quite a timid dog, and they're the ones I find the most interesting. I'd go in and sit in his enclosure and cuddle him,' Serena says. Being adopted by a loving family was exactly what Chopper deserved.

Leaving Dominic to take care of the paperwork, Romy returned to work, excitedly telling her colleagues about the new family member. Then, just as she sat down at her desk, her phone rang. It was Romy's youngest son, Rocco.

'Chopper's gone missing,' Rocco told her. 'He's run off!'

Romy's heart sank. 'Put your dad on the phone,' she said grimly.

'That was when our eleven-day nightmare began,' says Romy.

Chopper had indeed run off. Dominic and the children had made the 25-minute journey home from Lort Smith with their new pet being showered with love in the back seat all the way. But when they pulled into the driveway and the kids clambered out of the car, Chopper saw his opportunity.

'The kids got out and left the back door of the car open, and Chopper just jumped out and bolted,' Romy recalls. 'I was beside myself: how could you leave the car door open?! Dominic said, "I underestimated the dog – I was in Arthur mode!" Arthur would have panicked if he was ten feet away from us. He was never a flight risk, ever. He was attached to us from the moment we got him.'

But it was becoming abundantly clear that Chopper was not Arthur.

Dominic charged after Chopper until he lost sight of him, then raced home to get the car and continue the pursuit. Meanwhile, Romy rushed home from work and started scouring the surrounding streets on foot. It wasn't long until she spotted Chopper reassuringly close to home – but she couldn't get near him.

'He was crossing back and forwards across a four-lane road. There were cars screeching and two people tried to grab him,' she says. Their efforts were fruitless; frenzied Chopper just kept running.

Within hours, Romy had plastered the streets of Glen Iris with lost-dog flyers, and the search party was growing in number. Neighbours and friends combed the area for any sign of Chopper until nearly midnight, while a frantic Romy called virtually every vet, pound and animal shelter in Melbourne.

'Then we got a sighting and I thought, *great!*, but when we got there, there was no sign of Chopper,' she says.

It was the first disappointment in a rollercoaster of a search that would last nearly two weeks.

'You know that dog you gave me an hour ago? We've kind of lost him.'

As awkward telephone calls go, they don't get much worse. But if Romy expected recriminations when she rang Lort Smith's animal welfare officer, Jacqui Boyd, that Thursday to confess that Chopper had fled, she was in for a big surprise. Instead of judgement, Jacqui, Serena Horg and their Lort Smith colleagues immediately swung into action to help with the search.

Jacqui called in friends from rescue groups and they hit the streets. They would become the unofficial night shift for the duration of the search, driving around looking for Chopper until midnight or even 3 a.m. every night. Joining Jacqui that first night was colleague Mary-Anne Sanders. The next day, Mary-Anne signed herself off on annual leave so that she could spearhead Lort Smith's daytime search efforts.

'Jacqui and Mary-Anne were the two main, full-time dedicated people. They just didn't stop looking,' says Serena.

When she wasn't out looking for the elusive dog herself, Serena manned Operation Find Chopper's Lort Smith HQ, updating the social media pages that had been set up to spread the word about the search, fielding phone calls, and managing the not insignificant task of coordinating more than fifty volunteers.

'This was the first time we'd done anything like this. It was pretty sensational,' she says. 'The hardest part was trying to keep everyone informed. Everyone wanted constant updates, especially when there were sightings. Sometimes I had to stop looking and just sit and answer phone calls and emails. Then I felt guilty because I wasn't out there looking.'

The most frustrating thing about the search effort was that there *were* sightings of Chopper – lots of them, in fact. But they all led nowhere. Every time someone got close to Chopper, he would slip away like a ghost. A giant, furry ghost, with a sprinting ability to rival Usain Bolt.

'I was getting text messages constantly about potential sightings,' says Romy. 'All the people in the area were out looking for him. We had a sighting from a little boy who saw him running up a laneway and thought *brilliant!* But then nothing.'

The day after Chopper disappeared was a Friday, and Romy's day off. She spent the entire day in her car looking for him, stopping everyone she passed to hand over a flyer and plead for any information.

'I stopped one woman and said, "Have you seen this dog?" She said, "Yes! He's just round there,"' she recalls. 'So I raced off and saw this man running with his own dog and said, "Have you seen Chopper?" And the man said, "I'm chasing him!" But he got away again.'

Saturday saw a huge search party of family, friends, Lort Smith staff and even complete strangers fan out across the eastern suburbs. Not one person saw Chopper all day. On the Sunday, he was spotted crossing the Princes Highway at Malvern East at least three times. There was an army of volunteer searchers in the suburb, but they simply couldn't find him.

Then there was a reported sighting at the train station in the next suburb, Ashburton. For Romy, this was grave news. If Chopper was travelling east, he was heading towards densely populated neighbourhoods with lots of traffic and several major roads, including the Monash Freeway and busier sections of the Princes Highway.

But then another twist: Chopper was seen in Murrumbeena, 5 kilometres south of Ashburton. If confirmed, it would mean Chopper had miraculously managed to cross the busy, four-lane High Street.

The next sighting, in Murrumbeena's Boyd Park, was heartening. 'It's like a wilderness in the city, and a guy had seen him there half an hour earlier. We thought, *Okay, it's not that big – if he's in there we'll get him*,' says Romy.

They didn't get him, but the sighting was a revelation nonetheless. Boyd Park is a long, narrow reserve that runs between Murrumbeena and neighbouring Hughesdale. It's part of a linear park network that helps to give Melbourne's east its leafy reputation. The next link in the park chain is Malvern East's Urban Forest, then the Malvern Valley Public Golf Course, which connects to Ashburton along the Anniversary Trail Linear Park. But the golf course also connects with Darling Park, which merges with Dorothy Laver Reserve, which joins Glen Iris Park – not far from the Panzeras' home.

Suddenly, Romy understood how Chopper continued to evade capture. He was steering as far away from people as possible by hiding in the parks. The canny canine was following his very own green highway.

The Pakenham train line is a busy one. During the weekday morning commuter peak, trains rumble along the 56 kilometre track from Pakenham, on the edge of the West Gippsland region, to Southern Cross Station, in Melbourne's CBD, every ten minutes. Add to this the V-Line services linking downtown Melbourne with regional Victoria, and empty trains heading into and out of rail yards on both the Pakenham and adjoining Cranbourne lines, and Metro Trains driver Jane Evans had plenty to think about as she pulled her fully-laden train out of Murrumbeena Station on the Monday morning after Chopper absconded. Seeing a dog on the track was the last thing she needed.

'A train had just passed me on its way into town and I was leaving Murrumbeena, heading out to Pakenham. As the train passed me I saw a dog on the side of the tracks. He seemed stuck between the tracks and the fence,' Jane says.

She immediately slammed on the brakes. A lifelong dog lover herself, she knew that a scared, disoriented canine was just as likely to run towards danger as away from it. She passed the dog slowly, watching to see which way he would go. She thought he looked frightened and disheveled, and he seemed to be limping. As Jane's train slowed and eventually stopped, the dog crossed the tracks behind it and stood in the middle of the rails adjacent to hers.

'That image is seared into my memory,' she says. 'Looking into my mirror and seeing this dog standing on the train tracks, me knowing full well that a train was coming and that I couldn't do much about it. If a dog can look disoriented, then this one did. He seemed very confused as to how he had gotten there.'

Her train had stopped too far from the dog for her to be able to get out and go after him, even if that was allowed. Drivers are prohibited from using their radios to talk to each other unless there's an emergency involving other trains or people. But her train had come to a halt in front of the approaching city-bound service, and Jane was determined to alert the other driver to the doggy drifter ahead.

'A wandering dog doesn't rate very highly on the importance scale to the people who run the network so I had to think of another way to warn other drivers. I made all these crazy hand gestures, trying to tell the driver of the city-bound train that there was a dog on the tracks ahead, or at least to try to get the driver to slow down as there was something going on up ahead to be careful of.'

Though she had done all she reasonably could, Jane felt 'pretty stressed' by the time she reached Pakenham. One of the hardest aspects of the job, she says, is seeing the daily toll of animals that haven't survived their attempt to cross the train tracks.

'A possum or bird near the line is crappy, but a dog is heartbreaking for me. My dog means the world to me, and I assumed there would be a frantic owner searching for this dog somewhere. As soon as I saw him on the tracks, my heart sank,' says Jane.

On the return journey, she kept a watchful eye out for the dog in the Murrumbeena area. Seeing no dog – and importantly, no dog's body – she breathed a sigh of relief. The forlorn hound must have made his way off the tracks without incident.

Two days later, however, Jane's cousin shared a post about a missing dog on Facebook. As it happens, her cousin is good a friend of Serena Horg. The missing dog was Chopper – and Jane knew from one glance at the picture that Chopper was the dog she had spotted on the train tracks earlier in the week.

Immediately, Jane shared Chopper's 'missing' poster to a private Facebook group for Metro Trains drivers, urging them to keep their eyes peeled for him on the Pakenham line. She was driving the line herself that day, and was on high alert for any sign of Chopper. Then, when her shift finished, Jane drove back to Murrumbeena and, in pouring rain, started searching herself.

'I parked my car and went for a wander around the area, through the parklands and as close to the train line as I could safely get. Train drivers are suspicious of anyone who walks too close to the tracks, and I didn't want to get anyone's attention,' she says. 'I needed to search because I felt like I was doing something. I hate sitting around and waiting for things to happen.'

During her sodden walk, Jane bumped into Lort Smith's Mary-Anne Sanders, who was also looking for Chopper and re-attaching posters that had become unstuck. 'After that drenched conversation with Mary-Anne, when we were both soaked with tears and rain, I realised I was in too deep not to follow this search through. I was quite familiar with the area and the train line, and I felt I might be able to help. If my dog was missing I would move heaven and earth to find him. I couldn't turn a blind eye.'

Jane promised to keep searching, and took Mary-Anne's phone number so she could check in for updates. And she was as good as her word, returning to hunt through the area after work every day, often in torrential rain as the notoriously cold Melbourne winter took hold.

It didn't take long, she says, for the wet weather to become oddly soothing. 'When there is something important to do, a little rain shouldn't stop you.'

A week had passed since Chopper vanished. The tireless search efforts of more than fifty people had proved futile.

More than 71 000 people had viewed the Facebook page and posted upwards of 5000 comments. But every avenue they pursued lead to a dead end, and every sighting had come to nothing. The Panzera family was struggling. Romy hadn't slept in days, but the children were taking their dog's absence hardest of all.

'The kids instantly fell in love with Chopper at the dogs' home. Rocco had a complete meltdown. His grandmother had died just a couple of months earlier and he held it together then, but when Chopper went he collapsed,' she says. 'Aoife was devastated and cried herself to sleep for days.'

Privately, Romy was starting to lose hope of ever finding Chopper. 'I had said to Dominic, "I don't know about this, it's not good." Chopper didn't have a homing instinct, so he didn't know where to go. We weren't home to him yet, so he wasn't interested in trying to find us.'

On Thursday, a full week after Chopper disappeared, Romy had stayed home from work to care for Valentino, who was unwell. There had been a sighting in Oakleigh, about 7 kilometres south-east of Glen Iris, and then one in the vicinity of North Road, another major arterial thorough-fare, which runs in the opposite direction, west, all the way to the beach. The North Road sighting had been phoned in by a council ranger, and at first Romy wasn't convinced. It seemed impossible that Chopper could have successfully negotiated so many heavily trafficked roads. But the description matched Chopper to a tee, so Romy bundled Valentino into the car, and off they went once more.

'I said, "You can be sick in the car – get in, we're going!"' Then I made him get out and walk across Oakleigh Golf Course in the rain. We'd figured out Chopper was following parkland, so I dragged my sick son around most of Thursday and Friday. We were constantly in the car, driving everywhere we could think of, to no avail,' she says.

But the North Road sighting was encouraging for two reasons. Firstly, it showed Chopper was clever enough to safely cross major roads and, secondly, it seemed to suggest he was travelling west towards the ocean.

'When he started getting into the beachside suburbs, we thought that was good. If he was heading for the beach he'd have to stop when he got there, because where else was he going to go?'

Romy's only hope was that if he *did* make it to the beach, someone would be able to grab him before he disappeared again.

The next day, Saturday, the family left the morning search to the army of volunteers so that they could attend Rocco's soccer finals, planning to resume the hunt in the afternoon. After the match they joined Rocco's teammates for a celebratory McDonald's lunch, where Romy updated their parents on Chopper's apparently interminable journey.

'There were about half a dozen mums at the table and I was filling them in on the story and how awful it was and how horrible I'd been to my poor husband,' she says. 'And I was also telling them about how amazing people had been, and how people had stopped me in the street to tell me stories about their own dogs.'

But her dramatic tale was interrupted by a phone call. It was Serena Horg, and she was crying. Romy's heart leapt into her throat.

'I didn't want to call you until I had him in my hands,' Serena said.

Romy turned to the other mums at the table, wide-eyed, as she said: 'You've got him?'

'We've got him.'

All along, Serena had been joking that Chopper was trying to find her. She lives in the beachside suburb of Elwood, and on the Friday night before he was finally found, she had 'an eerie feeling' that Chopper was close by, going down to Elwood Beach to look for him. 'I just had a gut feeling that he was there,' she says. 'I concentrated my search around the Elwood Life Saving Club's barbeques, thinking he could be scavenging for scraps.'

As it happened, she was less than 20 metres out: Chopper was found at the other end of Elwood Beach on Saturday morning. The good Samaritan who found him took him to Elwood Veterinary Clinic, virtually opposite the beach, and said they had found him sitting on the sand, staring wistfully out to sea as if pondering the meaning of life.

One of Romy's friends was a client of the clinic, so the vets on duty were very familiar with the story of The Great

Chopper Chase and recognised him immediately. They called Lort Smith and Serena immediately raced over. As soon as she was satisfied that this was indeed the fugitive hound, she called Romy.

'I just burst into tears in McDonald's,' Romy laughs. 'About four of the other mums at the table started crying, too. Rocco was running around telling all his friends. It was like all his birthdays and Christmases combined.'

Train driver Jane Evans was also ecstatic to hear Chopper had at last been found. 'I could actually feel my whole body relax. It was like both my body and my mind realised I didn't have to stress about Chopper anymore,' she says. 'Knowing he was safe and alive was wonderful.'

Chopper's eleven-day journey had taken him 15 kilometres from Glen Iris to Elwood Beach, but based on the zig-zag pattern of sightings, it's believed he may have walked up to 50 kilometres. As far as those involved in the search can deduce, he stuck close to Glen Iris for most of the first week before beginning his pilgrimage to the beach, following the parks as much as possible, and when they ran out, tracking his way along the railway line. His paws were badly blistered, he was exhausted and he had shed about 8 kilos from his 46 kilogram frame, but the incessant rain during his ordeal fortunately meant he had avoided dangerous dehydration.

First thing Sunday morning, the Panzera family made the trip to Elwood to bring their new pet home for the second time. The Lort Smith brigade had also turned out in force for the reunion. 'I just couldn't wait to see him. It was very emotional, and there were a lot of tears shed,' says Romy. 'We left with him on a leash this time, obviously!'

But while Chopper's physical odyssey was over, his emotional journey was just beginning. When he finally made it to Glen Iris and his new home, he was a nervous wreck. While Romy, Dominic and the children had grown to love Chopper in absentia, to him they were complete strangers. All he knew was life at Lort Smith, and prior to that, long, lonely days starved of affection.

'He didn't know how to sit. He didn't even know how to play, not even with other dogs. This poor dog had just had no attention,' says Romy. 'We had to reinvigorate him and teach him how to be a dog.'

The first step was bestowing him with a new, more fitting name. Chopper was a tough, intimidating moniker; it didn't suit this giant, timid puppy at all. They finally settled on Fergus, an Irish name that means strength – a quality the tenacious wolfhound had proved he possessed in spades.

Strong though he was, Fergus suffered from terrible separation anxiety. The first time the family went out without him and left him in the garden, they came home to find their flyscreens shredded and the sides of their weatherboard cottage festooned with deep scratches two metres high, where Fergus had jumped up to try and get in the windows. He has improved with time and consistent training, and can now enjoy his own company three days a week. He also attends doggy daycare once a week. He was initially also fearful of men, but over time his bond with Dominic has deepened.

The family also quickly discovered that Fergus is highly intelligent. Within the first week, he had learned to sit, stay and drop on command. He can also twirl, and even open doors and window shutters. He adores his three human siblings, and personally greets each child every morning.

Slowly, and with the aid of the Panzera family's unconditional love, Fergus is blossoming – just like Arthur did before him.

'After two days we saw his tail wag for the first time, and my heart melted. I thought, *Here we go, we're onto a winner*,' says Romy.

No doubt Fergus was thinking exactly the same thing.

HOME FOR CHRISTMAS

PENNY'S STORY

Penny peered through the windscreen into the twilight. Nothing she could see out there looked familiar. The rocky, sagebrush-dotted flats that surrounded her home were long gone. Instead, beyond the arrow-straight freeway, a thin blanket of snow covered barren fields that stretched all the way to the darkening horizon. Penny could smell the cold.

She turned away from the window and fixed her gaze on the man at the wheel. Every now and then he lifted one hand and waved to the drivers of the semi-trailers that went thundering by in the opposite direction. Sometimes he smoked cigarettes, and they made Penny's nose tickle and burn. Often he grabbed at the small box that hung from a cord above his seat, hooting and hollering into it. There would be crackling and hissing, and then voices would come hollering back. None of the voices sounded like Colt or Kendra.

'Where are you taking me?' Penny tried to ask the man, but he didn't seem to understand her. 'I want to go home!' He just bellowed at her to 'stop your whining!' In its cradle on the dashboard, his mobile phone went *ping!* and *bzzzz* every few minutes, the eerie blue light of its screen illuminating the dim cabin. The man never picked it up.

As darkness gathered and the outside chill seeped in, the eighteen-wheeler rumbled on. Penny had never felt so alone.

Kendra Brown wasn't ready for a dog. She and husband Colt had been married less than a year and she was content to enjoy life with just the two of them for a little longer yet. Colt, however, was certain the time was right to welcome a four-legged family member. He helped run his family's onion farm in Royal City, Washington, 250 kilometres south-east of Seattle, and loved the idea of having a canine companion roaming the property beside him.

So Kendra relented, on one condition: this dog would have *boundaries*. It wasn't going to shed fur everywhere and sleep on the sofa and take over their lives. It was going to be the most well-behaved, drama-free dog ever.

Famous last words.

After extensive research, the couple decided on a Hungarian vizsla. The handsome breed is believed to have originated in Hungary in the tenth century, but has only been in the United States since 1950 and wasn't recognised by the American Kennel Club until 1960. Known for being athletic, fearless and protective, vizslas were prized by the Magyar tribes as hunting dogs – which appealed to Colt, a keen pheasant hunter. But they are also sensitive, gentle and affectionate, and they have a great affinity with children, which makes them great family dogs.

Despite her initial reluctance, it was Kendra who found the puppy they would name Penny. 'The vizsla is a popular breed and puppies are hard to come by. I had told one of my coworkers we were looking and she said, "One of my friends breeds them and she's just had a litter,"' she says. 'I called her, but she said the puppies were all spoken for.'

Disappointed but not discouraged, Kendra found another local breeder who was happy to add her name to the waiting list for a puppy from a future litter. It was June 2014, and it looked like the earliest she and Colt would be able to bring a pup home was October. They resigned themselves to a long wait.

'Then, at the end of July, my coworker called and said her breeder friend had had a puppy returned, and if we wanted we could come and see her,' Kendra says. Without telling Colt, she went to meet the little dog – who was then called Abbie – and instantly fell in love. She was house-trained and crate-trained, and seemed utterly perfect. Kendra wanted to take Abbie home right away, but the breeder sensibly insisted on keeping the puppy overnight to make sure there were no major physical or behavioural problems that had prompted her original owner to hand her back.

'The next day the breeder called and said, "She's just a great dog, and if you want her you can come get her." I tied a pretty pink bow on her and came home and gave her to Colt.'

Colt was also instantly smitten. 'I was like, *What's wrong with her?* since she'd been returned by her original owner, but there was nothing,' he says. 'I think he had a day job and when he got home and this puppy was all over him and into everything, he just wasn't prepared.'

That wasn't a problem for Colt, who immediately started taking Penny – her new name inspired by her deep copper coat, the same colour as a penny coin – to work on the farm with him every day. 'She'd ride with me every day – she'd be at the door in the morning waiting for me, ready to go. She'd run around a lot, and I'd get her pretty worn out by the end of the day.'

Onions are grown on the farm during the summer months, then harvested, packaged and shipped all over the world in winter. By December 2014, six-month-old Penny was spending less time romping around in the fields and more time in the packing shed.

'Our packing shed is really in the middle of nowhere, down a dead-end road. We call it the badlands. I'd leave my door open when I was in the shed, because I didn't want Penny just sitting in my office all day,' says Colt. 'She'd go out for maybe thirty minutes, then come in for some water or food. She would always check in.'

Friday, 19 December, was a particularly busy day in the packing shed. Colt was on his feet all day, hustling to fill the spike in orders that always came with the Christmas rush. Around 3 p.m., he suddenly realised he hadn't seen Penny for a while. He checked his office, but she wasn't there. He looked in and around the shed; she was nowhere to be seen.

'I asked some of the men who work for us, "Have you seen my dog?" They all know her, but they hadn't seen her.'

Colt called Kendra, who immediately left work, and together they searched high and low for Penny until well past midnight. 'I could hear coyotes howling all night, and I was thinking, *I'm sure they've got her*,' he recalls. 'I should have taken better care of her.'

Kendra was equally frantic. 'She was just a six-month-old puppy. She was so little. I was worried she'd gotten hurt and lain down somewhere and we just couldn't see her.' It was also freezing cold, and the single-coated vizsla is not at all equipped for being outside in icy temperatures.

The next day, Saturday, the couple searched desperately for Penny from dawn until dusk. 'We drove around and put signs up all over town, but there was no sign of her at all,' Colt says.

The Browns also took to social media, asking their respective Facebook friends to share Penny's photos and information in the hope that someone local may have seen her. Kendra also posted appeals for help on any animal rescue page she could think of. But when they finally fell into bed that night, she and Colt felt hopeless. There hadn't been a single sighting of Penny since she went missing. She couldn't have got far on her little legs; how was it possible that nobody had spotted her?

'That night around 11 p.m. we were lying in bed and I got a text message from a rescue group saying, *Check out your Facebook page*,' Kendra says. 'I logged in and saw that a lady had commented: *I saw her on Friday afternoon – a truck driver was calling her, but he didn't know her name*.'

The woman worked at the cherry plantation directly across the road from the onion packing shed. Like Colt's farm, the cherry orchard was a hive of activity in the lead-up to Christmas Day, with delivery trucks constantly coming and going. The woman had braved the frigid winter temperatures for a five-minute cigarette break, and had seen Penny wandering around. She had also seen a truck driver trying to coax the little dog into his cab.

It was the breakthrough Colt and Kendra had been hoping for. First thing Monday, Colt went to the cherry plantation and got a list of all the trucks that had been there on Friday. The worker who had seen the man calling to Penny was able to narrow the list to the truck she thought was his. Colt got on the phone.

'The first company I called, they put me through to their dispatcher. I talk to trucking companies all the time, so I know the lingo. I said I wanted to talk to this driver about his load,' he recalls. 'The dispatcher said, "I can't give out his personal number, but I'll get him to call you."'

Colt hung up and settled in for an anxious wait. Would the dispatcher really pass on his message? And if he did, would the driver call? Colt wanted to give the man the benefit of the doubt. Surely he had a good reason for driving off with his dog. Then again, what if he didn't even have Penny? Maybe she scampered off into the badlands after all.

Within minutes, Colt's phone rang. 'I said, "Did you happen to pick up a dog?" and he said, "Yeah! She's sitting right next to me in the cab of my truck,"' he says. 'I told him, "That's my dog!" and he said, "Oh sorry, I thought she was a stray and I was going to take her to the nearest shelter or police station."'

Colt couldn't help but feel dubious. The driver had picked Penny up on Friday afternoon and now it was Monday morning. He hadn't managed to find a shelter or police station in almost forty-eight hours? Still, Colt was relieved. At least he knew now who Penny was with, if not *where* she was, so all he had to do was go and get her.

'I'm thinking, *This is great, I'm going to get my dog back*. So I said, "Where are you now?" and he said, "Nebraska."'

Penny was 2100 kilometres from home.

'Colt called me and said, "Let's just drive to Nebraska!"' says Kendra. 'I said, "Let's calm down and think about this before we get on the road."'

In the four hours since Colt had made contact with the trucker, the situation had gone from odd to absurd. Colt asked the man to take Penny to the nearest shelter, and said he would speak with them directly to arrange her return. The driver said he would.

He didn't.

When Colt spoke to him again a little while later, he was unapologetic. 'I'm in an eighteen-wheeler,' he snapped at Colt. 'I can't just stop on the side of a small city street.'

Though his patience was wearing thin, Colt still wanted to believe the driver really did want to see Penny returned to him. 'In my mind I was thinking, *He says he has Penny, which he wouldn't admit to if he was stealing her, so he has to cooperate*,' he says.

Colt asked the driver where he was next planning to stop. He figured he could find a rescue group there, call ahead and arrange for Penny to be picked up. That was when the man started to lose his cool. 'He was saying, "I'm in the middle of nowhere, this is not my problem!"'

He also pleaded with the couple not to tell his employer what was happening; he was afraid he would lose his job. Colt wasn't planning to involve the trucking firm – yet. But it helped to know he had a bargaining chip up his sleeve. The way things were going, it looked like he would need it.

Another hour dragged by without further contact. Sixty torturous minutes in which Penny travelled 100 kilometres further from home and Colt was ready to take off in pursuit of his puppy. But Kendra urged caution, because she was concerned the trucker might harm Penny if he felt threatened. She couldn't bear to imagine what might happen to her if the helpless puppy was dumped by the side of the interstate in the ice-cold Midwest.

Finally, the driver called again. He was still heading east. He told the couple his final destination would be Green Bay, Wisconsin, some 2800 kilometres from Royal City. Kendra sent out an appeal on Facebook: *Does anybody know anybody in this area who can help us pick up our dog?* The response was immediate, and a 'Penny pick-up team' was soon ready and waiting in Green Bay.

'We got a few things lined up,' says Kendra, 'and that was when he went silent.'

The afternoon stretched into evening. All of Kendra and Colt's calls to the driver went unanswered, until a brief conversation late that night.

'The last time I talked to him he said he was in Des Moines, Iowa,' says Colt. 'He said his co-driver was at the wheel and he'd be sleeping, "so don't call or text me and wake me up."'

Des Moines was 2700 kilometres from Royal City, and about 700 kilometres from Green Bay, where the driver had said his journey – and Penny's – would end. If they were going to drive all night, they would reach Green Bay, on the shores of Lake Michigan, well before daybreak. It was imperative Colt and Kendra talked to him again to coordinate Penny's handover to the volunteers they had lined up there.

'We woke up every two hours and called and texted him through the night, but got no response,' says Kendra.

When Tuesday dawned with no update – and knowing it was well past the time Penny should have arrived in Green Bay – Colt felt he had no option but to play his trump card. 'Eventually I thought all I could do was threaten him, because I knew he didn't want to lose his job,' he says.

He dialled the driver's number again, and again it went straight to voicemail. Colt left a message, telling the man he was going to call the trucking company. Its fleet is tracked, he said, so his employer would know where the man was.

'About a minute after we left that message, he sent a text message back saying, *I dropped off your dog at a truck stop in Des Moines*,' says Kendra. 'He went on to say he'd given Penny to another driver travelling west, and that this driver would call us.'

Kendra's worst fear had been realised. If the trucker could be believed, Penny was now in the hands of yet another stranger – or worse, the tiny puppy had been left to fend for herself beside an eight-lane highway.

'We said we needed some more information,' she says. 'What was this driver's name? What was his phone number? He said all he knew was that he was called CJ and that he drove for Swift, which is America's largest trucking company.'

Scant though the information was, at last the couple felt there was a light at the end of the tunnel. Desperate for answers, Kendra set up a Facebook page, 'Bring Penny Home for Christmas.' It amassed more than 20000 followers within a day, and Swift was soon being inundated with calls from concerned supporters appealing for the company to help track 'CJ' down.

'We were thinking we just had to wait for this guy to turn up in Washington and call us,' says Kendra. 'We'd been on quite an emotional rollercoaster at this point. We thought Penny was gone, then we found her, and then she was gone again.'

But the rollercoaster was about to take another devastating dive. Kendra and Colt also called Swift, which has a fleet of more than 100000 trucks on the road across the United States. Incredibly, the company was able to pinpoint seventeen vehicles that had been near Des Moines around the time the driver said he'd handed Penny over at a truck stop. That was as far as their assistance went, however. Two days before Christmas, the Swift juggernaut was in full swing. The company simply didn't have the time or resources to try and locate the mysterious CJ.

It was another frustrating dead end.

With a hiss of its hydraulic brakes, the big rig groaned to a stop. Penny sat up on the passenger seat and blinked the sleep from her eyes. Through the window, she could see a squat brick building with a big blue sign. On the sign was the silhouette of a dog.

The driver swung his door open and jumped down to the pavement. Then he lumbered around to Penny's side of the cab and wrenched open the passenger door. She cowered in her seat. Was he going to shout at her again?

But no. He picked her up and lifted her down from the truck, took her to a patch of grass near the building's front door. She squatted and relieved herself. It had been a long, *long* time since she'd last had the chance. She'd been worried she would have to go on the seat, and she knew he wouldn't like that.

The man picked her up again and carried her into the building. Penny blinked furiously as her eyes adjusted to the bright lights inside. The scent of other dogs was overwhelming. *What is this place?* she wondered. He set her down on the linoleum floor. She liked the sound her toenails made as she skittered across it, her nose on the ground, sucking up as many of those intriguing smells as she could.

The truck driver stomped to the counter at one end of the bright room. A lady in a blue tunic sat behind it.

'Found this dog,' he said gruffly. 'Dunno who it belongs to.'

The lady came out from behind the counter and picked Penny up. She scratched under Penny's chin as she carried her into another room and set her on a shiny metal table. Soon, a man came in holding a big plastic paddle. He waved the paddle over Penny's back and it gave a loud *beep!*

'Great,' said the man. 'She has a microchip. I'll make the call.'

*

It was 11:30 on Wednesday morning, Christmas Eve. Colt was at work, but he couldn't concentrate on the job. He couldn't concentrate on anything, for that matter, except where his dog was. Penny had been missing – held hostage, more like – for six days. Bringing her home for Christmas was looking like an increasingly remote possibility.

Then his mobile phone rang. Colt peered at the screen. It was a number he didn't recognise. He should have known better than to hope for another call from the trucker. *Area code 412*, Colt noted. *Where the heck is that?* He answered the call.

It was someone calling from Banfield Pet Hospital, saying, 'We had a dog come in and we scanned her microchip and your information came up – when can you collect her?' His stomach flipped. He said, 'That's great! Where are you?'

The reply left him speechless. 'They said, "We're in Pittsburgh."'

Pittsburgh is 3800 kilometres from Royal City. It is the second-largest city in Pennsylvania, the truck driver's home state. He had given his name and address to the staff at the vet clinic when he took Penny in, having taken her on a week-long transcontinental journey.

He had never been headed for Green Bay. There was no 'CJ', no Des Moines truck stop. From the moment he enticed Penny into his eighteen-wheeler in the parking lot of a Royal City cherry orchard, he had fed Colt and Kendra a pack of lies.

'Maybe he just thought he'd bring this nice little puppy home for Christmas for his family,' Kendra says. 'But Colt had said to him, "She's chipped, so if you ever take her to a vet they'll find out she's ours."'

Maybe the driver's conscience got the better of him. Maybe he lost his nerve. Maybe spending six days in a tiny truck cabin with a boisterous six-month-old puppy quickly lost its appeal.

'Penny loves to run, so being in that truck for so long – she probably wasn't a very good dog in there. I can imagine she'd have wanted out so bad,' Kendra laughs. 'It is a miracle that he didn't lose her. I'm sure that he probably wasn't very nice to her.'

But the couple's joy at the news that Penny was at last safe was tempered when clinic staff told them they would be obliged to send the little dog to the pound – or worse, hand her back to the truck driver – if her rightful owners couldn't collect her. Strangely for a thief who was frightened of losing his job, the trucker had remained at the vet hospital, ready to take Penny back if Kendra and Colt couldn't make other arrangements for her.

Now the Browns were in a race against time to get their voyaging vizsla back to Washington. Penny's incredible journey wasn't over yet.

Kendra's first call was to the Pittsburgh Police Department. She explained the situation – that her dog was poised to be handed over to the man who had stolen her – and pleaded with them to collect Penny from Banfield Pet Hospital and keep her until arrangements for her return to Royal City could be made. She was stolen property, after all – couldn't they seize her? Being Christmas Eve, Kendra's main concern was that everything would shut down for the holidays and poor Penny would be left out in the cold once again.

She also contacted several local animal rescue groups, and in the midst of wrangling with the police department received a call from a woman who was eager to help.

'She was going, "Okay, I'm in my car, I'm turning right, I'm on my way!"' says Kendra. 'She went and picked her up from the vet for us.' Kendra understands that the truck driver only left the clinic once the rescuer arrived.

Next, the Browns received a call from Pittsburgh's Bureau of Animal Care & Control. The county dog warden was on the case. 'He got involved and helped transport Penny to a shelter that could hold her over Christmas,' she says. 'We got her all transferred on Christmas Eve, and she stayed there until Boxing Day.'

What should have been their first Christmas with their canine companion was bittersweet for Kendra and Colt. They'd had plans to celebrate with Kendra's family in her hometown of McCall, Idaho, but cancelled those plans when they thought they had to be available to meet the mysterious 'CJ'. Once they knew Penny was being well cared for – albeit almost 4000 kilometres away – they did travel to McCall for a belated Christmas celebration. 'We figured all the phone calls and travel arrangements could be done from Idaho,' she says.

Penny's story had made the news all over the country. Friends of Kendra's in Idaho, 800 kilometres from Royal City, even overheard people in a restaurant discussing the puppy's journey. Plenty of people reached out to the couple over Christmas, suggesting myriad ways to get Penny back to Washington. A pilot offered to fly down to Pittsburgh and personally fly Penny home, while a dedicated vizsla rescue group they'd found online wanted to arrange a cross-country carpool.

'I said, "Thank you, but no – after what she's just been through I'm not trusting her to thirty different drivers!"' says Colt.

The couple knew they would need to do something drastic to bring Penny home, and toyed with the idea of driving to Pittsburgh to collect her themselves. But before they could formulate a solid plan, fate intervened once more.

Shortly after the bizarre tale aired on the nightly news on Christmas Eve, 'We got a call from the regional Vice President of Alaska Airlines, who said, "We heard your story and we'd love to fly Penny home for you free of charge,"' says Kendra.

It was a touching offer, and one Kendra and Colt eagerly accepted, although like everything else that had happened over the past week, it wasn't straightforward. Alaska Airlines doesn't fly out of Pittsburgh, so there were a few more moves to make yet.

Nevertheless, Colt and Kendra were finally able to relax; they were going to be able to bring their girl home.

'Once she was with the dog warden in Pittsburgh, I think we were able to trust that she was safe. Before that, we weren't really sure that we'd get her back,' Kendra says. 'Once she was at the shelter we felt like there was an end in sight, even if it meant we had to get in our car and drive to Pittsburgh!'

A vizsla rescue group collected Penny from the animal shelter and placed her with a foster carer for a week. She had contracted worms and kennel cough during her unscheduled stays at the shelter, and had to have a clean bill of health before she could fly.

'This family had another vizsla, so Penny played and had lots of fun,' says Kendra.

Then another vizsla enthusiast drove Penny from Pittsburgh to an experienced breeder ninety minutes away. The breeder had lots of experience transporting dogs by air and had volunteered to deliver Penny to the airport in Baltimore, Maryland, the closest Alaska Airlines hub, and see her onto the aircraft.

Finally, on 2 January 2015 – fifteen days after free-wheeling Penny hit the road – she touched down in Seattle, a two-and-a-half-hour drive from Royal City. 'We were getting texts from the pilot saying, *We've got Penny onboard and we're about to take off!* He also texted us when she landed. It was awesome,' says Kendra. 'They were willing to do whatever it took to get her home safely.'

Penny had lost weight, but was otherwise well and in exuberant spirits. 'She was a little sickly and it took her a few days to get back to normal, but she remembered the house and the yard,' she says.

Kendra and Colt are understandably extra vigilant about Penny's whereabouts these days, especially at the farm. 'We have a lot of trucks that come into our packing facility, and I always keep her with me until they're gone, because you just never know,' says Colt, who in a remarkable act of festive goodwill, never reported the truck driver to his employers.

And those rules the couple were adamant Penny would follow? They were significantly relaxed following her ordeal.

'She wasn't allowed on the couch until she got stolen, but now she can do what she wants,' Kendra laughs. 'This was definitely a surreal situation. You hear of these strange stories, but I would never have thought it would be something we'd go through.'

While she has stuck close to home ever since, it seems her odyssey did give Penny a taste for the open road. 'Colt's mum bought a motorhome recently, and Penny just got up in the passenger seat and sat there like she was about to take off on a road trip,' says Kendra.

Wherever her next adventure takes her, one thing is for certain: Kendra and Colt will be by her side. She is, after all, their lucky Penny.

PIPE DREAMS

JAY'S STORY

South Australia's capital city, Adelaide, has a reputation as a genteel, oversized country town known for its churches, arts festivals and award-winning wineries. But travel 25 kilometres north of the CBD's wide streets, historic buildings and verdant parklands, and things are a little different.

Adelaide's northern plains are the city's working-class heartland, a flat, featureless landscape dotted with market gardens, public housing and light industry. The area may not be able to boast the white sandy beaches of suburbs to the south and west, the mansions of the affluent east, or the fertile green hills of wine country further north, but this is a place that's proud of its blue-collar roots; a place where people stick together and there's nothing you wouldn't do for a mate.

They breed them tough out north – and none tougher than an eleven-year-old bull terrier mix called Jay.

Chris Jones has had Jay since she was fourteen months old. She first belonged to a friend of Chris's who had assisted at Jay's birth and was rewarded with a puppy from the litter. But when his friend's work commitments meant the precocious pooch with the big brindle spot over one eye was forced to spend long, lonely days alone, Chris decided to give her a new home.

It wasn't a tough decision; in fact, it seemed like fate. 'I've known Jay from day one and I just knew she was a brilliant dog,' says Chris. 'Everything pointed towards me taking her on.'

From the moment Jay moved in, she and Chris have been inseparable. Then working as a truck driver, he would load his four-legged travelling companion into his rig and off they'd go on journey after journey, exploring the country together.

Everywhere they went, Jay attracted attention. If people weren't remarking on her powerful, muscular build or her gleaming white coat, they were marveling at her manners. 'She's the sort of dog that's responsible and behaved enough that you can take her places. She's well mannered and polite,' Chris says proudly. 'Everybody that meets her says what a good dog she is. Everyone loves her.'

But people would jump to conclusions, too. They would assume Jay was male, or that she was aggressive, simply because she looked like the stereotypical 'tough mutt'. Nothing could be further from the truth, says Chris.

'She's a tough looking dog, but she's a pussycat. She's an angel, in fact. She's super smart, and she's as loyal as you could ever imagine a dog to be. She's the best dog I've ever seen in my life, and I've been around.'

A decade passed, and the pair's bond only grew deeper. Theirs was a happy, quiet life made all the richer for their devotion to each other.

Most days, Chris and Jay would travel from their home in Parafield Gardens to Happy Home Reserve in nearby Salisbury, where she could run off-leash till her heart was content. Bisected by the Little Para River, and with the Salisbury North Wetland in its north-east corner and the outdoor pools of the Salisbury Swimming Centre on the southern side, the large, grassy park is as popular with picnickers and young families as it is with dog owners.

The reserve is also home to a feral cat population, and one of Jay's great joys during her daily walks was to chase the vagrant felines. 'She'd never catch them – it was just the thrill of the chase,' Chris says. 'She loved it – she'd have a huge grin from ear to ear.'

That's just what Jay was doing on the afternoon of 27 May 2015, when her incredible journey unexpectedly began.

It was a stunning late autumn afternoon: it hadn't rained for weeks and the sky was a deep, cloudless blue. On their way to Chris's weekly Wednesday eight-ball game with friends – where Jay was always welcome, naturally – they stopped at Happy Home Reserve so she could burn off some of the energy that belied her advancing years.

Chris stood back and watched his beloved dog run and run. Jay would disappear for minutes at a time, but would return periodically to check in, pink tongue lolling and panting heavily.

'She popped up again and I said, "You've got five more minutes and then its time to go," like you'd say to your kids. She is like a little kid to me,' he says.

Five minutes later, cheeky Jay predictably hadn't returned, so Chris set off to round up his recalcitrant hound.

There was no sign of her.

He shouted her name over and over again. Nothing. The only sounds were the birds in the wetland and the roar of traffic on busy Salisbury Highway and Waterloo Corner Road, which border the park.

It just wasn't like Jay to disappear. In ten years, she'd gone AWOL just once, when a balloon burst in Chris's living room and a startled Jay bolted for the door. That day, thanks to her microchip, she had been home within hours 'like a remorseful teenage runaway'.

She had a strong personality and could be stubborn at times, but Jay always came back. *Always*. She loved Chris too much not to.

Growing increasingly frantic as he combed the park, Chris called the friends he was due to meet for his eight-ball game to tell them he wasn't going anywhere until he'd found his girl. 'The instant I rang them they said, "Right, eight ball is cancelled, we'll see you there in five minutes,"' he recalls. 'Straight away, they were there.'

The search party scoured every corner of Happy Home Reserve, staying long into the night. Chris was distraught, calling Jay's name with a voice thick with tears.

But it was no use.

Jay had vanished.

It was dark, so dark. Just a moment ago she'd been sprinting in the afternoon sunshine. Now Jay couldn't even see the tip of her shiny black nose.

Uh-oh. I might be in trouble here. Where's the sun gone?

She looked to the left, then to the right, but there was only inky blackness in every direction. She tried to spin around, to retrace her steps. *I'm a smart dog, I can figure this out.* But even that was a struggle: her backside was wedged against a cold, hard surface, and so was her face. She had to twist her neck at an extreme angle to make the turn, and when she finally did there was nothing ahead of her but night.

Jay sniffed the air. The atmosphere in the cramped space was stale and damp. She could smell wet dirt, rotting vegetation and – *sniff, sniff* – the faintest whiff of the wily cat she'd pursued in here.

Hmm, Jay thought. *This is no good. I'd better go find Dad. He can't be far away.*

And so, following her nose, she set off slowly into the void.

*

Something was niggling at Chris. There was a nagging thought in the back of his mind, and no matter how hard he tried to dismiss it, no matter how often he told himself, *Jay just wouldn't do that*, he couldn't shake it.

What if Jay had run into the stormwater pipe?

In the part of the park where the feral cats liked to congregate was an outlet pipe, maybe half a metre in diameter, that discharged stormwater into the Little Para River. Chris had often looked at it and wondered where it led. As a young boy growing up in Elizabeth, about 10 kilometres further north, he and his mates had fancied themselves as thrill-seeking subterranean explorers. They'd take their torches and crawl into the local stormwater pipes, exploring as far as they dared before hightailing it back to daylight.

'You'd go up a certain way and look back and it'd be dark. Everywhere you looked, pitch dark. Disorientation would come on very rapidly,' he says.

Jay had often looked at the pipe in Happy Home Reserve too. Chris would spy her nosing around its entrance and with a sharp 'no' send her on her way. She knew the pipe was off limits. She'd never be brave – or silly – enough to venture inside it, would she?

'She'd poke her head in there, but she'd always back out. I'd always wondered whether she'd chase a cat if it went up the pipe, but I didn't really think she'd entertain the idea. I always thought, *That'll never happen*,' says Chris. 'Famous last words.'

And if she had chased a cat into the pipe, then what? If Chris, armed with a torch and lashings of boyhood bravado, had found the experience disorienting and frightening, how would Jay cope with being lost, alone and *way* out of her comfort zone?

Salisbury City Council's drainage network comprises more than 400 kilometres of underground pipes and is serviced by more than 14000 side entry pits (kerbside drains) and junction boxes. The pipe diameters range from 30 centimetres to 2 metres; in and around Happy Home Reserve, the smallest pipe is 45 centimetres wide and the largest 90 centimetres. Could Jay really be inside that labyrinth? And more importantly, could she get out?

It seemed preposterous, but the other scenarios Chris turned over and over in his mind were no better. Jay had been gone for nearly twenty-four hours now and he had already plastered the area with 'missing dog' posters. If she was still in the park, why hadn't he found her? If she had escaped into the surrounding streets, why hadn't there been any sightings? If some well-meaning person had picked her up, thinking she was alone in the park, why hadn't they since returned her? The thought of Jay being struck by a car on Waterloo Corner Road or Salisbury Highway was too awful to contemplate, and anyway, Chris had already called all the local vets and pounds.

There was a possibility that she'd been stolen, he conceded; there had been a recent spate of dognappings in the area. But somehow Chris knew that wasn't the answer. In his heart, he truly felt Jay had gone into the stormwater pipe.

He went to the council and told them of his concerns. He wanted a full-scale search launched for his girl: 'I wanted the State Emergency Service (SES) on the case, I wanted helicopters in the sky. I was prepared to put my Rambo uniform on and go up that pipe myself. I will do absolutely anything for this dog.'

But Chris says council staff told him it was highly unlikely Jay was trapped in the stormwater system, and of course they couldn't deploy council resources to look for a lost dog. There are more than 25 000 registered dogs within the Salisbury city limits; imagine if council staff were obliged to leap into action every time one of them went wandering.

So Chris was back at square one. His best friend was gone. All he could do was keep searching, and keep hoping.

Jay was so tired. Hungry, too. How long had it been since she'd had anything to eat? But mostly she was cold. There was no sunshine down here and it was absolutely freezing. Even when she squeezed herself into one of those strange tiny spaces where she could see a sliver of daylight not far above her head, it didn't do much to warm her up.

Sometimes she saw feet up there in the daylight. Not paws like hers, but people feet – like Dad's. When she saw them walking past she barked and yelped and howled as loudly as she could. 'Hey! I'm down here! Will you help me?' But nobody heard her.

At least she wasn't thirsty anymore. For a long time – hours or days, she didn't know – Jay's mouth had felt as dry as a desert. She dreamed of her water bowl at home and felt herself growing weaker. She wondered how much longer she could keep going. Then it rained.

It rained for days and days, and she drank as much as she could and felt stronger. But the water swirled around her, rising higher and higher. It swept sharp things and heavy things and tangle-you-up things past her in the dark, scratching her skin and bumping into her with a thud. The water made Jay feel even colder, and she couldn't find a dry place to sleep. It was tougher than ever pushing her way up the narrow tunnels that never seemed to end.

Jay had never felt so lonely. She longed to go home. But she wasn't afraid. Her dad always told her she was the smartest girl in the world. She knew he'd never give up on her, and that made her feel strong and hopeful.

All she had to do now was find him.

Chris was exhausted and distressed. In the three weeks since Jay disappeared, he had run himself ragged trying to bring her home. His campaign to find his dog had rapidly gathered momentum, with Jay's image being shared widely on social media. The posters he'd wallpapered throughout Salisbury and the surrounding suburbs had led to a deluge of phone calls from people who believed they'd seen Jay; Chris personally investigated every one of them, but still hadn't been able to confirm a single sighting. It seemed everyone knew about Jay, but no one knew where she was.

Not content to simply sit and wait for Jay to turn up, Chris continued to comb Happy Home Reserve and its surrounds for any trace of her.

'I was traipsing through places I would usually never even consider going. I walked up and down dry creek beds. I ran through spider-infested weeds. I have an incredible fear of anything creepy-crawly, but I went head first into the Salisbury North wetlands,' he says.

'I went back to the park every day, looking and calling for her. I even went and stuck my head in the stormwater pipe. I knew Jay was a strong dog, and I knew to keep looking.'

After the dry first week, May turned into June and winter arrived, bringing with it four days of heavy rain. Although the temperature plummeted, hovering in the teens during the day and dipping into single digits at night, Chris was relieved. He knew Jay could survive on meagre scraps of food if she had to, but he was terribly worried about her prospects if she couldn't access fresh water.

'That was a huge weight off my mind. I'd been praying for rain and I had to say, "God, thank you for that, because now she's got water and that's one less thing I have to worry about."'

Chris couldn't bring himself to cross any place or possibility off his list unless he'd checked it out himself. That was why, on 17 June – three weeks to the day since Jay's vanishing act – he climbed wearily into his car to follow up on a reported sighting of Jay at the Parafield train station, about 5 kilometres from Happy Home Reserve.

As he drove down Salisbury Highway, fully expecting to be disappointed once again, Chris's phone rang.

'Mate,' said a man's voice at the other end of the line. 'We've found your dog.'

Chris felt his heart sink. How could this bloke have Jay if she was at the train station? One way or another, he felt he was about to crash headlong into yet another brick wall.

He told the caller he was on his way to another possible sighting, and that he'd get there when he could.

'No mate,' the caller was insistent. 'This is *your* dog. You need to get down here now.'

Suddenly, Chris heard a yelp in the background. Tears filled his eyes. He'd know that yelp anywhere.

What's that sound? Marie closed her car door and turned her good ear toward Waterloo Corner Road, struggling to hear over the rush of the afternoon peak. She was certain she'd heard something, but what was it?

Clutching her dogs' leashes tightly this close to the busy road, 83-year-old Marie walked slowly across the car park in the direction of the sound. Her pets pulled in the opposite direction, eager to race off into the adjacent dog park for a run, but they would just have to wait. She may be hard of hearing, but Marie was sure she wasn't imagining this.

There it was again! A distinct yelp, high pitched yet muffled – and it seemed to be coming from the stormwater drain set into the gutter. Marie quickened her pace, crouched down low and peered into the drain's rectangular opening, just 20 centimetres tall.

A pair of eyes shone back at her.

Jay was squashed into a space the size of the average household freezer, covered with a reinforced concrete slab and more than 2 metres deep.

Marie waved down a man aged in his twenties, Keith Nitschke, who happened to be walking past on his way to the local shops. Together with another man who had spotted the commotion from the dog park and run over to help, the trio heaved the concrete cover off the drain.

Though her white coat was filthy and she was painfully thin, the man from the dog park recognised Jay immediately. This was the dog on all the posters! Her broad doggy grin had been staring out at him from tree trunks and light poles for weeks. He raced back into the park, snatched the nearest flyer and dialed the phone number on it.

Meanwhile, young Keith had clambered down into the drain pit and hoisted Jay out. He carried the weary dog to Marie's car and prepared to lay her down across the back seat. At least she'd be safe now; the last thing Jay's rescuers needed was for the poor dog to get spooked and bolt again before her owner arrived.

They didn't have to wait long. Moments later, Chris's car came screeching into the car park. He'd been close by when he received the call, and his initial hesitation to believe Jay had really been found had quickly morphed into frenzied elation.

'The tone of the man's voice on the phone was adamant – he knew they had found Jay. The clarity and seriousness in his voice, saying "You should come now," made me believe it,' Chris says.

When the caller described where he'd found Jay, Chris was convinced. 'I knew exactly where he was talking about, because I'd poked my head into that drain days earlier. I can't describe the feeling.'

As Chris drove into the car park, he saw Jay cradled in Keith's arms. The engine had barely stopped running before he leapt out of the car and embraced his dog.

'I looked at Jay and as soon as she saw that it was me, you could see the weight of the world just completely lift off her shoulders. I could see it in her eyes – the relief was awesome,' he says. 'She would have seen the same thing when she looked at me. I just cuddled her and cried.'

Miraculously, Jay emerged from her ordeal mostly unscathed. While she had lost an enormous amount of weight and was very weak, Jay was otherwise uninjured. After a veterinary check up, Jay all but inhaled a one-kilo can of gourmet dog food, and then finally Chris was able to take her home.

'She came home, sniffed around all her places and her beds, jumped up on the lounge and went into a deep, deep coma-like sleep,' he says. 'She'd wake up every now and then to check that I was still there, but she slept for days and days.'

As the flood of emotions gradually subsided, the extent of Jay's journey and the improbability of her discovery in the roadside drain began to hit home. Chris doesn't consider himself a particularly religious man, but he believes divine intervention played a part not only in Jay's survival, but in elderly, partially deaf Marie hearing Jay's exhausted whimper from a dozen metres away over the sound of hundreds of passing cars.

Jay was found just 500 metres from where Chris believes she chased a feral cat into the stormwater pipe and got lost. She had spent twenty-one days wandering in a 400-kilometre-long network of pitch-dark underground tunnels, but somehow she had followed her nose – or her heart – back to virtually the exact spot she disappeared from.

The same spot Chris had returned to every day looking for his best mate.

'When she came out of that drain she was on the cusp of death. She was knocking on heaven's door,' he says. 'The vet said she might have had one more night in her. Somehow she had the energy for one last bark, and amazingly someone heard her.'

Chris often wonders what went through Jay's mind during those long, lonely days trapped beneath the ground. He doesn't much like telling the story of Jay's incredible journey; thinking about it still gives him goosebumps and he says both he and Jay are ready to move on.

'I can only imagine what it was like for her, what she was thinking and how she survived. I look into her eyes still today and think, *How did you do it?* She just gives me a look as if nothing ever happened,' he laughs.

'I've worried about the trauma of it all, but it doesn't seem to faze her in the slightest. She just hasn't missed a beat. It's an incredible story, but that's Jay – she's an incredible dog.'

Her tough appearance may hide a gentle nature, but there's no doubt Jay has the spirit of a warrior. When asked what he thinks kept Jay going for those three frightening weeks, Chris pauses before answering: 'Loyalty.'

Whether he means Jay's loyalty to him, or his to her, doesn't really matter.

SOMEONE TO
WATCH OVER ME

TILLIE AND PHOEBE'S STORY

It may be just a stone's throw from downtown Seattle, but Vashon Island maintains a folksy rural charm that makes it feel a world away from its cosmopolitan neighbour. Spanning an area of less than 100 square kilometres, the island is a haven for artists and outdoor enthusiasts alike; a melting pot where organic farmers rub shoulders with the members of the resident opera company at the local gluten-free café.

Accessible only via a 22-minute ferry ride across Puget Sound – the *New York Times* called the voyage 'a trip across water, and time, from Seattle' – Vashon's 10 000 residents vehemently opposed the planned construction of a bridge to the mainland in 1992. That small-town feel, and the islanders' passion for preserving it, is part of what drew BJ Duft to Vashon Island in October 2011.

As the owner of Herban Feast, a successful catering and events company based in downtown Seattle, BJ admits he works constantly. He started his hospitality career in hotels and spent more than a decade working in big cities before taking a job at a renowned restaurant in a tiny town 40 kilometres east of Seattle. He found the peace and quiet of the countryside so charming that, when he launched his own business back in the city, he wasn't prepared to give up that bucolic lifestyle. He wanted to spend his rare downtime surrounded by natural beauty and friendly faces rather than concrete and a sea of smartphone screens. He also wanted his dog, an Irish setter–spaniel cross called Tillie, to have plenty of space to run around.

Vashon Island seemed to tick all the boxes. It's the sort of place where everyone knows everyone, and where parents don't think twice about letting their kids play in the woods until dark – and all within easy reach of Seattle.

And as BJ soon discovered, Vashon Island is also sort the sort of place where people keep an eye out for each other's dogs.

Tillie had been an 'only dog' for more than five years by the time BJ bought his 5-acre 'farmette' on the island. He had adopted her as a puppy in 2004 to be a playmate for his golden retriever, Stella.

'One of the vendors that I buy seafood from for my business knew I was looking for a dog and let me know that his dog had had puppies. I wanted a companion for Stella because I work constantly, so I wasn't at home as much as I wanted to be,' he says. 'I went over to his house and of course all the puppies were super cute, but I just fell in love with Tillie because she had such a sweet nature.'

Sadly, just a couple of years after Tillie joined the family, her best friend Stella was diagnosed with cancer and passed away. BJ didn't think about becoming a two-dog household again until 2013, when Tillie was nine. She certainly didn't seem to be wanting for company. When BJ was at home, Tillie was his shadow, and when he went to work she spent her days at a doggy daycare centre in Seattle, where she had plenty of four-legged friends.

In fact, Tillie had one friend there that she was particularly fond of: her canine BFF, Phoebe.

'I really wasn't looking for another dog, but the woman who owns the daycare place told me her brother had to give up his basset hound. She kept telling me, "Oh, she and Tillie are the best of friends, you should think about adopting her,"' says BJ.

Eventually, he agreed to take the two-year-old basset hound home for a week-long trial. 'Of course, I fell in love with Phoebe too, and I could see she and Tillie were inseparable,' he says.

From the start, Tillie and Phoebe have been devoted to each other. They share everything, from their beds to their food dishes. 'Tillie never had puppies, so I feel like it's a mother–daughter connection. They're very "lovey" with each other, although Phoebe can be very bossy with Tillie,' says BJ.

Their bond is all the more extraordinary given their very different characters. Phoebe, the young upstart, is playful, energetic and mischievous. Thanks to her keen sense of smell – the bassett hound's scenting ability is second only to the bloodhound – she's happiest when she has the freedom to follow her nose.

'My property is all fenced, but if I ever leave the gate open while I'm unloading groceries, Phoebe watches me and if she thinks I'm not paying attention she runs for it. If she smells a squirrel or a deer, she just goes. Those squat little legs can move!'

Tillie, on the other hand, has a more genteel sensibility. Like her owner, she appreciates the calm and quiet of the countryside. 'She's very docile and has a very soft disposition. If I'm watching something and I holler at the TV, she goes to another room and cowers,' says BJ. 'She's not a wanderer. She likes to stick close to home. Tillie would never leave the property of her own volition.'

Such is Tillie's fealty to Phoebe, however, that she has always gone along for the ride when her curious companion has set off in search of pastures new. The pair once discovered – or created – a hole in the property's boundary fence and enjoyed three or four outings before BJ managed to find and repair it. On each occasion, the dogs either made their own way home by dinnertime, or were picked up and returned by a helpful local.

'Generally Tillie would tire out because she's older and she'd just go to somebody's house. They'd call me saying,

"I have your setter" and I'd say, "Great, where's the bassett hound?"' says BJ.

That's why he wasn't especially worried when Tillie and Phoebe performed their Houdini double act once again on 7 September 2015.

The day before, a Sunday, BJ had hosted a company party at his home. More than 300 employees and vendors had attended the bash, and he'd had to remove a section of fence to allow the large trucks carrying all the necessary equipment and supplies to get in and out. His sister, Christy, was staying with him at the time, and when he left for work on Monday morning he forgot to mention to her that the fence had yet to be replaced.

'I was heading into Seattle and Christy was coming home and we waved to each other as we passed. It didn't dawn on me to tell her I hadn't yet closed the fence up, so she just let the dogs out, thinking nothing of it,' BJ says. 'Fifteen minutes later she was texting me, just freaking out.'

The dogs were gone. Phoebe had spotted the gateway to freedom and made a break for it, with Tillie going along to keep an eye on her rascally offsider.

His sister may have been frantic, but BJ wasn't overly concerned. An hour or so after their escape, a neighbour spotted the dogs just a little way down the road. They ran off into the woods before they could be rounded up, but at least BJ knew roughly where they'd be.

'Of course I was worried because I didn't want them to get hit by a car or attacked by another dog, but I wasn't as stressed out as I might have been if they hadn't been spotted,' he says. 'I knew they would stay together, and I thought they'd go off on a trail and end up at somebody's house.'

When he returned from work that evening, BJ grabbed a torch and went out searching. His first stop was the thicket Phoebe and Tillie had been seen disappearing into – they weren't there. Nor were they anywhere else he looked that night, and no one had glimpsed the elusive pair since the neighbour's sighting that morning.

On Tuesday morning, BJ called local vets and animal shelters, as well as everyone else he could think of on the island who might have seen the girls. He put 'lost dogs' posters up all around town. Still, he thought it was just a matter of time until Phoebe and Tillie emerged from the woods and made their way home.

'Vashon is not a big island – it's just 22 kilometres long – but there's lots of woods and trails. I thought they'd just dashed off and were having a heyday,' he says.

By Wednesday, however, he was starting to feel uneasy. 'After two days, when nobody had seen anything, I started to feel a little anxious. When they'd disappeared before, they'd been back within hours. This was a weird circumstance because, aside from that first sighting, we just never saw them again.'

Sharing his concern was Amy Carey, a volunteer with Vashon Island Pet Protectors (VIPP), a not-for-profit, no-kill animal rescue organisation. BJ had first spoken to Amy when he called VIPP to see if Phoebe and Tillie had been brought in, and she was keen to launch a more intensive search for the pair.

'I didn't want to panic, but Amy gave me a reality check. She told me the dogs could be in a well or in a ravine,' he says. 'She was telling me not to worry, but also trying to prepare me for the worst-case scenario.'

Settlement of Vashon Island began in 1824, and the earliest inhabitants built open wells to access groundwater and cisterns to catch and store rainwater. With the advent of closed wells most were covered or filled in, but there are still dozens dotted around the island, often hazardously concealed by the dense woodland.

The island's undulating landscape can be challenging for dogs, too. It includes steep, narrow gorges, rushing creeks and a sphagnum bog, plus countless fallen trees left behind by the island's early logging trade. Vashon is also home to coyotes, raccoons, and even the occasional black bear that swims across from the mainland – any of which could cause real problems for an elderly setter or a low-slung bassett hound. And while the island is small, its roads can be busy, teeming with tourists and daytrippers throughout the summer.

BJ got the picture. With the help of Amy and VIPP, he rallied search parties to scour the island for any sign of the dogs. They hunted for a full week, following up on even the vaguest of leads and combing what felt like every inch of Vashon Island.

'There were three teams of us heading into different areas across the island. We were relying on people saying, "I think I saw a couple of dogs . . ." Whatever lead we got, we just ran with it,' he says.

But it was all for naught. Tillie and Phoebe, it seemed, had vanished into thin air.

There were dogs as far as the eye could see. The usually green fields of Misty Isle Farms were today a sea of mostly black and white fur; border collies and other herding breeds brought in from all over the country for the renowned Vashon Sheepdog Classic. Many of the 8500 spectators had brought their dogs, too. Spotting Phoebe and Tillie among this morass of wriggling, wound-up canines would be almost impossible, like a giant canine version of *Where's Wally?* Still, BJ was certain they would come. They just had to.

Catering Vashon's annual sheepdog trials is a big job for BJ's company, Herban Feast, but it's also something of a treat for him. The hugely popular three-day event is staged just across the road from his home, so it's a quick journey to work and a fun few days out. And this year was sure to be extra enjoyable, because if anything could lure Phoebe and Tillie out of hiding, it had to be hundreds of dogs and the tantalising scent of food right on their doorstep.

'The event was about dogs, with dogs, and everybody brought their dogs. I kept thinking they'd smell the food and come running right across the field,' BJ says. 'I would finish up at the end of each day and go straight out to look for them.'

It wasn't to be; nobody had seen the dogs for days.

Tillie and Phoebe had been missing a full week now, and their absence had really begun to hit home. 'I was thinking that if I didn't find them I would move off the island, because I couldn't bear the thought of living out here with the dogs gone,' he says.

Then, on Monday, 14 September, VIPP's Amy Carey received a phone call.

'A community member said he saw a dog for the past few days coming up to his property, come up near him but not all the way, and then going back down a trail to a ravine behind the house,' she told America's *ABC News*.

Amy immediately set out to investigate, calling BJ on the way. 'I was on one side of the island and Amy was on the other,' he recalls. 'She said, "Somebody said they saw a red dog over here, so why don't you come and we'll canvass the area?"'

The red dog could certainly have been Tillie, but the tip-off was worrying. Tillie never willingly went any-where without her partner in crime. If it was her, then where was Phoebe? Still, it was the most promising lead they'd had yet, so BJ jumped in his car and headed off to meet Amy.

He was nearly at the rendezvous point when Amy called again. This time she said, 'They're here! They're here!'

Amy had gone to the caller's house and followed a snaking trail from his backyard into a ravine about 6 metres deep. It was the same path he said he had seen the mysterious red dog tread. When at last she reached the floor of the ravine, Amy called Tillie's name and heard a single 'Woof!' in reply. She raced in the direction of the sound, and couldn't believe what she saw.

There, at the bottom of a concrete cistern almost 2 metres deep, a glum looking Phoebe cowered. And standing guard over her was Tillie.

'I was overwhelmed. I just felt so relieved and elated when I got the news. I pulled up and ran out of the car and into the woods, and I hopped right into the cistern with Phoebe,' says BJ.

While he can't know for sure how Phoebe ended up in the cistern, which had been partially filled in, he suspects she jumped in for a drink of water after her daring flight from home, only to discover her short little legs couldn't make the leap back out.

'She can hop up onto the kitchen counter to get food though,' he adds dryly.

He believes Phoebe was stuck in the cistern for most – if not all – of the week she and Tillie had been missing; he's certain she would have come home or been spotted otherwise. The dogs were just 3 kilometres from BJ's property, but they'd travelled in the opposite direction to their previous jaunts. They had even managed to cross Vashon Island's main highway.

What BJ *does* know for sure, however, is that devoted Tillie had kept watch over her best friend the entire time. She had made the difficult journey out of the craggy ravine, with its deep holes, fallen logs and thick bush, every day for a week in her desperate quest for help. The man who spotted Tillie and called VIPP said she had run out of the woods and barked urgently at him on at least three occasions.

'He didn't know it was Tillie; he thought it was a neighbour's dog. I think she wanted him to follow her in,' says BJ.

Amy Carey is equally sure that Tillie was maintaining a vigil for Phoebe. 'It was very clear what Tillie had done,' she told *ABC News*. 'She had not left her friend's side except for going up to the man's house when he was there to try and get help for Phoebe.'

Navigating the terrain could not have been easy for an ageing, frightened dog, but tenacious Tillie did it again and again. 'I was slip-sliding going down there to get to them, so it was a feat for her, and then she had to make sure she could find her way back to where Phoebe was,' says BJ.

He wasn't at all surprised to realise Tillie had stayed by Phoebe's side. 'The fact that they stayed together was amazing. If Tillie had wandered off, we would never have found Phoebe, and we'd never have known what happened to her. I want to hope that Tillie knew that, and that's why she stayed.'

Though both dogs were ravenous and exhausted after their ordeal, neither was injured or dehydrated thanks to the water in the cistern. BJ believes Tillie must have jumped down into it to drink – but unlike Phoebe, she was able to scramble out again.

Within an hour of arriving home, Phoebe seemed to have shaken off the trauma of her excursion and was playing with her favourite toy, a tennis ball. 'I got them home, then let them outside and was going around the property with them, and where does Phoebe go but right back to where the fence was open. That just told me what she was all about,' BJ laughs. 'She has the biggest backyard ever – why does she feel she needs to leave?'

He later installed an invisible fence, which gives a small shock when a dog tries to pass through it, but even that couldn't contain Phoebe's wanderlust. 'It was up on the highest setting and she just shook her ears and walked through it.' Now she wears a collar with a GPS locator instead.

Tillie, on the other hand, is less inclined to leave the house these days. Now eleven, she seems to feel she's seen quite enough of the big, wide world.

News of Tillie and Phoebe's incredible journey spread across Vashon Island in what felt like a matter of minutes. And then it kept spreading around the world. A Japanese magazine even proposed having an animal psychic 'interview' the dogs in the hope of finding out what really happened during their journey.

Washington governor Jay Inslee later presented Tillie with a 'Washingtonian of the Day' award, and there is an unofficial push on Vashon Island to have her elected mayor.

(The island doesn't actually have a mayor, so it's a major accolade indeed.)

Tillie was also named as a finalist in the 'Dog of the Year' category in the inaugural World Dog Awards. BJ, Tillie and Phoebe were flown to Hollywood for the ceremony. Tillie didn't win, but as they say, it was an honour just to be nominated.

'During the announcement of her category, Tillie and Phoebe were asleep at my feet,' says BJ. 'They didn't even care.'

The interest in Tillie and Phoebe's story was intense. And while BJ understands the interest, he says it was overwhelming at times. 'I think people were so fascinated by it because we often think dogs aren't as smart as us, or don't have the same attachment to and care for their dog buddies, so people are like, "Wow, a dog did this for her companion?"' he says. 'But I didn't expect this level of interest. It was one little thing on a blog, and then all of a sudden it was a frenzy of news stories. I was more embarrassed, like, *Oh my god, these dogs have gotten out again. People must think I'm a horrible pet owner!*'

Slowly, however, the fanfare subsided and life on sleepy Vashon Island returned to normal. Tillie dotes on Phoebe as much as ever, while Phoebe's gratitude to her friend hasn't tempered her bossiness. What's changed the most, says BJ, is his relationship with his remarkable girls.

'I think my connection to them is different now. It's easy to take things for granted, but when you almost lose something and you're able to get it back you cherish it a bit more,' he says. 'I'm just so grateful to have them in my life.'

THE HOMESICK
HOBO

PERO'S STORY

At first glance, there was nothing particularly remarkable about Pero the Welsh sheepdog. A solid, reliable worker, the young collie-type canine was neither the best dog nor the worst on Alan and Shan James's farm near the tiny village of Penrhyncoch, near Aberystwyth in West Wales. He was good with the smaller flocks of sheep at the home farm – the acreage nearest the family house – but not as fond of travelling further afield to gather the big mobs. When there was work to be done close to home, Pero could always be counted on to leap up onto the quadbike behind Alan and head out into the fields. And unlike many sheepdogs, Pero also had an affinity for herding cattle. To his busy owners, Pero was a useful part of the furniture.

The James family has sixteen sheepdogs to help manage the 3000 sheep and sixty cattle on their 310-hectare farm.

The farm is also home to a pack of thirty-two Welsh fox-hounds that belong to one of Alan and Shan's three adult sons. Canine commotion is par for the course.

'All the dogs here are working dogs – none of them live in the house. The foxhounds have their own kennels and the farm dogs are either sleeping in the farm sheds, or they're in the back of Alan's Land Rover,' Shan says. 'We also have some retired dogs that happily sit outside on the doorstep.'

But while dependable Pero, who was born on the farm in 2011, may have been just another face in the crowd, he did have a few quirks that hadn't escaped Alan and Shan's atten-tion. In particular, Pero had a mischievous streak.

'Pero is not one of our main working dogs because he never enjoyed going with Alan in the Land Rover. When-ever Pero would go in the vehicle he would always fight with the other dogs,' says Shan. 'He would also go to the dogs in the kennels and antagonise them, make them all bark. And he was your classic postman-chasing dog. As soon as the van came down the road, he'd go for the postman.'

Pero also had a knack for getting under people's feet, and Shan admits he often made a pest of himself. 'Whenever Pero was about the place he was always in the way, so over the years I've always been the one to shout at him. I can't approach Pero; he's not a dog that comes to me. If I call him he'll wag his tail, but he won't allow me to touch him,' she says.

It's a different story with Alan, however. Though Alan has a farmer's typically businesslike relationship with his working dogs, Pero has always had a soft spot for the boss. 'Pero has always been more of a "one-man dog". Alan can approach him no problem. He shouts at the dogs too, but they always come back for more. They know who their master is,' says Shan.

It was Alan who gave Pero his name. Shan can't recall exactly where the name came from, but it was likely selected purely because it's a short, easy moniker to shout across a vast field filled with barking dogs and hundreds of sheep. It would turn out to be a prescient choice: Pero is a Greek word meaning 'rock' or 'stone' – something strong and steadfast, much like the dog himself.

As anyone who grew up in a big family can attest, it can be tough to stand out from the pack when there are numerous boisterous brothers and sisters vying for attention. Imagine, then, how difficult it must be to get noticed in a crowd of nearly *fifty* canine extended family members. Pero needed an opportunity to make his mark – and he was about to get it.

In March 2016, an acquaintance of Alan's got in touch and asked if he might be able to spare a sheepdog. The man knew of a fellow farmer in the Lake District in the northwest of England who was looking for a dog to work with small flocks of sheep.

Such a request was not uncommon – Alan and Shan's sheepdogs have a reputation as hardy workers, and they regularly loan or sell dogs to other farmers. 'We have puppies throughout the year from different bitches that we know are good dogs,' Shan says. 'Quite often we'll get enquiries, "Do you have a dog that does this or that?" That's how it is with farm dogs. Alan knows all their personalities, and knows which dog will suit the requirements.'

When his contact passed on the farmer's query, Alan immediately thought of Pero. 'This farmer wanted a dog that would work well in a "one man and his dog" sort of set-up, and Pero does prefer working with Alan and the smaller flocks rather than going out into a larger area,' she says.

It seemed like this could be Pero's time to shine. 'We thought, *He's five years old, he's ready to do more.*' It seemed like an opportunity for Pero to be his 'own person' – to move to a place where he'd be able to be himself instead of being in competition with all our other dogs,' Shan explains. 'So we said to this farmer, "Take him and try him out – you've got nothing to lose."'

On 22 March, Alan's acquaintance arrived to drive Pero the 400 kilometres north from Penrhyncoch to his new home near Cockermouth, in the English county of Cumbria. When it came time to leave, Pero wasn't keen – but Alan and Shan thought his reluctance had more to do with being confined to a travel crate for the four-and-a-half-hour journey than anything else. 'He did show signs of not wanting to go. We could tell he wasn't happy, but he was being pushed into a dog carrier to travel,' Shan says.

If Pero was instead sad to leave the farm, and Penrhyncoch, it wouldn't be surprising. The pretty village is in the north-western part of the historic county of Ceredigion, known for its rolling green hills, the craggy Cambrian Mountains, 80 kilometres of sandy beaches and the picturesque coastal hamlets dotting the shores of Cardigan Bay, the largest bay in Wales. Nearby Aberystwyth, where Shan grew up, is the county's largest town and a popular seaside resort during the warmer months. Ceredigion is one of only two places in the UK frequented by bottlenose dolphins. In other words, it's a natural playground – and an ideal home for a cheeky sheepdog.

With Pero off on his new adventure, life on the farm went on. Lambing season was in full swing and the James's remaining fifteen sheepdogs worked from dawn until dusk. With summer approaching, the days were growing steadily longer and Alan often made the most of the lingering light by working outdoors until eight o'clock.

But all was not well in Cockermouth. Pero's guardian kept Alan and Shan updated on his progress, and it seemed he wasn't settling into his new home.

'The farmer had told us that Pero wasn't happy. He wasn't connecting. They were keeping him in a kennel and he told us Pero seemed frightened in there, that he just stayed in the corner,' Shan says. 'We thought, *It's a new venture, just give him some time.* We suggested to the farmer that he let Pero out and give him a bit more freedom because he was so used to it, but the farmer was a bit wary of leaving him out because he didn't know Pero and didn't know what his traits were.'

Mindful of not expecting too much from his new charge too quickly, the farmer put Pero to work only once in the first couple of weeks. 'He took him out one day on the quad-bike but Pero didn't really do much,' says Shan. 'He did follow the farmer, though, and he came back no problem.'

On 7 April – seventeen days after Pero's trial stay in Cockermouth began – the farmer took Pero out to herd the sheep again. And that's when Pero decided he'd had quite enough of his new living arrangements.

'The last thing the farmer saw,' says Shan, 'was the dog carrying on across this forty-acre field – and beyond.'

Pero didn't look back.

At first, the farmer wasn't too concerned about Pero's vanishing act. It's not unusual for working dogs to get lost or go wandering on big properties, especially when the dog is new to the farm. They have an excellent sense of direction and invariably turn up. Besides, the farmer had been leaving food out for the missing collie each night, and the bowl had been empty each morning, so he figured Pero was hiding out nearby.

When two days passed with no sign of the stubborn sheep-dog, however, the farmer called Alan and Shan, mortified that he couldn't find the dog they had entrusted to his care.

'The farmer was worried because technically he'd lost our dog, but Alan wasn't worried at all,' Shan recalls. In fact, Alan shared the farmer's suspicion that Pero would be

lurking somewhere nearby. 'He said, "He's there somewhere, he's probably watching you from a distance." Alan
has experienced it himself, where he's lost one of the dogs in
a new, unfamiliar area of land – they go in the wrong direction and just keep going.'

Alan was extra confident that Pero would be found
because the dog had an identifying microchip. Microchip-
ping only became compulsory across the UK on 6 April – the
day before Pero ran away – and fortunately the Jameses had
already had their pack chipped. If someone other than the
farmer found Pero and took him to a vet, his microchip
details would lead home to Penrhyncoch.

Alan said to the farmer, 'Don't worry about it, he'll turn
up – and if he doesn't turn up with you, he'll turn up with
me.' He couldn't have known how prophetic his words
would turn out to be.

Another twelve days passed without a sighting of Pero.
In Cockermouth, the farmer continued to put food out each
night and woke to find an empty dish each morning. Meanwhile, in Penrhyncoch, Alan and Shan continued to wait for
news of their wayward worker, either from the farmer or
from a nearby vet.

On 20 April, a Wednesday, Alan returned from the fields
for dinner with Shan and the couple's youngest children,
eight-year-old twins Annie May and Tomos, around 8 p.m.
He ventured back out after eating to keep working in the
last of the evening light, but a moment later, he was back
indoors with astonishing news.

'He came in and said, "Pero is outside,"' says Shan.

It took Shan a moment to comprehend what Alan was saying. He couldn't possibly mean that Pero, the sheepdog that hadn't been seen for two weeks and was thought to be 400 kilometres away in Cockermouth, was in fact sitting on the doorstep – could he?

'I went outside to see and was saying, "Is this Pero? Are you sure?" Alan said, "Of course it is, don't you recognise him?"' Shan laughs. 'Alan knows his dogs, but it didn't click for me straight away. I thought it had to be a joke, that somebody had dropped him off. I was saying, "No way!"'

Pero himself was in no doubt he was in the right place. 'I could see the excitement in the dog. He was jumping up; he was very excited to see Alan. It was literally as though we'd just released him from the kennel,' says Shan.

But how had he got there? The possibility that Pero had spent a fortnight *walking* back to the farm after absconding from Cockermouth seemed too fanciful to contemplate. There had to be another explanation.

'I made Alan phone the fellow who took the dog up to Cockermouth because I didn't believe he could have just all of a sudden turned up,' she says. 'I made him phone him in front of me and then I had to speak to the fellow as well because he didn't believe *us*. We thought he was playing a joke and he thought we were in on the joke.'

It took some time and a flurry of phone calls to verify that Pero indeed appeared to have made it home under his own steam. 'It took a couple of days for it all to settle and to have it confirmed that the farmer in Cockermouth hadn't put him on a lorry and sent him back to us, or that the gentleman who took him up hadn't brought him home again.'

Pero was in relatively good shape given his 400-kilometre odyssey. He had lost a small amount of weight and his coat was dull and dirty, but he didn't have any obvious injuries.

'Before he went he was a very strong, square sheepdog – he wasn't quite as square when he came back,' says Shan. 'But he'd obviously found his way to food and there was a lot of rain on the journey, so he had water. He wasn't injured, but we saw in the days following his return that he was limping about the place.'

As the magnitude of his journey began to sink in, so did an insatiable curiosity: just how had Pero made it all the way home on his own?

Desperate to find out more about Pero's quest, Shan had a brainwave. She knew just the person who could help piece together the intrepid canine's movements during his two-week trek: BBC Wales journalist Sara Gibson.

'Sara is friend whose children go to the same school as mine and I just happened to mention to her one morning, a few days after Pero reappeared, "Is there any mileage for you in a story about a dog walking all this way?"'

Sara was fascinated and couldn't wait to write a news article about Pero's journey that included an appeal for anyone who may have spotted him along the way to get in touch with Shan.

The response to Sara's story was immediate and overwhelming. Faithful Pero's long journey home was reported by media outlets around the world, and the James family was soon being inundated with letters and phone calls filled with well wishes for the tenacious collie. He was even sent doggie treats through the post.

'It's taken us very much by surprise,' Shan says of the reaction.

And just as she had hoped, among the fan mail were messages from people who were able to help fill in the blanks of Pero's adventure.

First came a note from the wife of a sheep farmer in the small village Gressingham, about 130 kilometres south-east of Cockermouth near the English city of Lancaster. She believes she saw Pero on the night of 9 April, two days after he disappeared from the farm. As she wrote to Shan, she was alarmed to see an unfamiliar dog in the couple's fields, which were filled with young lambs:

> I looked out the window to see a collie dog going quickly through our sheep. My husband didn't see the dog at all, but I saw it going purposefully along the fence on the hill. It didn't seem interested in our sheep. For a second it was there and then it went off in a different direction and we've not seen it again. We've made extensive enquiries locally and no one has a dog like this one. It is possible the

dog we saw could certainly have been yours. The timing would have been right.

If the dog spotted at Gressingham was indeed Pero, it's likely he was sticking to the countryside that follows the A591, a pretty – and very busy – road that skirts some of the Lake District's most popular destinations, including Lake Windermere, Rydal Water and Bassenthwaite Lake. Perhaps Pero was taking in the sights on his way home.

The next sighting came three days later, on 12 April, when a couple thought they spied Pero heading towards Knighton, a small market town in the Welsh county of Powys. Knighton is about 240 kilometres from Gressingham, which would mean Pero had travelled a staggering 80 kilometres per day for three consecutive days. If the dog seen by the family was Pero, he had also overshot his destination – Knighton is 90 kilometres south-east of Penrhyncoch.

'He was spotted on the A488 from Clun to Knighton in a hamlet called New Invention,' says Shan. 'He's gone out of his way to get there, because it's not on the direct route.'

Said the letter writer:

> I may have seen your dog on his travels. We live in the Welsh Marches and on Tuesday, 12 April, I was driving home with my husband and our border collie. About 10 p.m. I saw in front of me two shining eyes, which turned out to be a collie trotting purposefully along the

verge. He looked tired and bedraggled. I've thought about this dog a lot since, hoping he got home safely.

It seems poor, disoriented Pero veered even further off track after that, because the next possible sighting of the homesick hobo was in a village near Worcester, a further 80 kilometres south-east of New Invention and 160 kilometres from Penrhyncoch.

'A woman phoned and said she was going through the village on her way home and this dog was loose, running through the village. She tried to catch it but couldn't, so she followed it in her car and cornered it,' says Shan. 'She could tell that he was scared so she dropped back a bit and he escaped. She said, "All that was on his mind was escaping from me." He ran off up a hill and through a hedge.'

It wasn't lost on Shan that, just like the two letter writers, the woman who called described the dog she'd seen as 'purposeful'.

'Her words were that he was "on a mission",' she says. It's a description that certainly tallies with Shan and Alan's experiences with their wilful, mischievous sheepdog. Pero had always had a mind of his own.

In hindsight, Shan says Pero's microchip was unlikely to have been of much use because he would have been almost impossible to capture. 'When I look at Pero, I can see that. From knowing that I can't even approach him, I doubt very much whether anyone would have been able to catch him.'

To her mind, there is no other explanation: Pero simply must have walked all the way home, dodging traffic and well-intentioned strangers, eating any scraps he could find and following whatever circuitous path his nose led him down.

'A lot of people say, "I just don't believe it." They can't accept that a dog has achieved such a mission,' she says. 'There's still an element of me that feels it's remarkable, but he actually did find his way home. I just wish he'd had a camera on him!'

But while the James family now has a better understanding of how Pero got home, and where his journey took him, exactly *why* he embarked on such a grueling expedition – why he was so determined to get home to Penrhyncoch – remains something of a mystery.

Shan believes Pero was simply homesick: he missed the farm, the only home he had ever known, and was more devoted to Alan than anybody had ever realised. 'All our dogs have bonded with Alan, and this breed of collie is very loyal to its master,' she says.

If Pero's goal was to set himself apart from his Penrhyncoch pack and prove himself an exceptional canine, he certainly succeeded. Now that he's home again, however, Pero seems content to resume his place somewhere in the middle of the pecking order.

'He's a little quieter than he was before, but he does still antagonise the other dogs. There are still dogs here that will pick on him, too. We've got a lurcher that doesn't like Pero very much,' says Shan.

All the media attention has also helped to improve Pero's people skills; he's a little more genteel in polite company these days. 'He'll come around to the front of the house a little more and stand at a distance, wagging his tail,' she says. 'If the door's open he'll come in the house because he's become used to being inside when we've been waiting for media outlets to come and take photos. We did a Welsh children's TV program and he was lying there on the lawn with Annie May, licking her to death.'

As for his short-lived stay in Cockermouth, Pero's opposition to that experiment has been well and truly noted – he won't be returning.

'We've got no reason to move him on again. He's happy here and at five years old he's fully working,' says Shan. 'He'll continue his life here, happily running around and enjoying his time with the other dogs.'

Because, after all, home is where the heart is.

THE LUCKY ONES

LUCKY AND BELLA'S STORY

Not all those who wander are lost. So wrote J R R Tolkien in his beloved fantasy novel *The Fellowship of the Ring*, and he was right. Some wander because they are found. They wander because they have the freedom to travel, the confidence to roam, the opportunity to experience the world alongside someone whose love is steadfast and unconditional. Some wander all the days of their life, and keep wandering in the next life, too. For some, like German shepherd mix Lucky and purebred boxer Bella, and their human, Michele Martin, the incredible journey never ends.

Michele wasn't looking for a dog the day Lucky came into her life in 1995, but Lucky definitely got lucky when her then owner approached Michele on the street in Denver, Colorado. It was a rainy morning, and Michele was feeling anxious and exhausted after being terrified by a prowler at her home the night before, when out of the blue a homeless man pleaded with her to take his beloved dog. The tiny ball of fluff was barely a year old; still just a puppy. He simply couldn't care for her, he told Michele, and she deserved better.

Michele was hesitant. Though she had felt a deep connection with dogs since childhood, she was just twenty and wasn't sure she was ready to assume sole responsibility for a dog, especially one that had already endured so much in her short life.

But seeing the man's desperation, and looking into the dog's soulful brown eyes, she felt she couldn't refuse. She agreed to take Lucky in temporarily – just until the man was able to get his life in order.

'I gave him my number and told him that if he could get on his feet he could have her back, but I ran into him a couple of weeks later and he was a mess. He had given up,' Michele says. 'I decided to try and rehome Lucky, so I found her a great place on a 200-acre farm in southern Colorado.'

But there was a problem. As the day of Lucky's journey to her new home drew nearer, Michele realised she couldn't part with the quiet, gentle dog whose grace and serenity belied her youth. Lucky was here to stay.

'Lucky was an old soul. She was always loving and forgiving, even as she had to deal with me growing from a kid with no real sense of how to raise a dog to a woman who had finally figured it out,' she says. 'She was always patient with me, always accepting. She watched me and helped me to grow up. In many ways she helped to raise me during those years.'

Lucky kept her watchful eyes on Michele for more than ten years, through moves to three different states, an engagement, relationship break-ups and even September 11. They spent eight months apart when Michele moved from Denver to New York City and struggled to find a pet-friendly apartment.

'Because Lucky had travelled to so many places with me, and because we were separated for those eight months, I promised her a visit to Cape Cod. That was always my promise whenever I had to leave her, that I would take her to Cape Cod,' she says.

Lucky also formed a strong bond with one of Michele's friends, Dieter. She loved going to work with him and adored his family, and so as she headed into her twilight years she began to divide her time, spending four or five days a week with Dieter and the rest with Michele. 'It was an odd scenario, but she had chosen him as her best friend so it was a great experience for her,' says Michele.

Then in 2004, ten-year-old Lucky began to behave strangely. Michele couldn't quite put her finger on it, but she knew something was off. She mentioned her concerns to Dieter, and after Lucky's next visit with him he agreed she wasn't herself.

'Dieter suggested we take her to the vet, and after hours of tests the vet told us she had a tumour in her heart. They suggested we euthanise her immediately.'

Michele was stunned. Lucky had a hemangiosarcoma, an aggressive, highly invasive form of cancer that occurs almost exclusively in dogs, and more so in certain breeds including the German shepherd. The cancer grows in the lining of blood vessels, and dogs rarely display any symptoms until the tumours spread or grow large enough to rupture the cells, causing fatal internal bleeding. Treatment for the disease can include chemotherapy or removal of the affected organ, which obviously wasn't an option for Lucky.

Michele knew her canine companion was gravely ill, but she couldn't bring herself to have Lucky put to sleep. Without treatment, veterinarians gave Lucky just two to three weeks to live. Michele vowed to make those weeks as wonderful as possible. After all Lucky had done for her, it seemed like the least she could do. But just as she had demonstrated time and time again during her eleven years, Lucky's spirit and love of life was not easily diminished. She had not come to the end of her journey just yet, and three weeks turned into three months.

'In the end I opted to treat her with diet and holistic medicine. We took it day by day, then week by week,' Michele says. 'I truly believe that the acupuncture, diet and supplements helped to give Lucky – and us, her people – three really great months.'

Sadly, while the hemangiosarcoma in Lucky's heart had stopped growing, the cancer had spread to her lungs. There was nothing more anyone could do. On 29 January 2005, Lucky let Michele know she was ready to go.

'She looked at me and Dieter, and we knew she was ready. I held her and whispered in her ear what a great dog she had been, while she held Dieter's gaze until the very end,' she says.

The weekend after Lucky's terminal diagnosis, Michele had at last been able to fulfill her promise to take Lucky to Cape Cod. Along with Dieter and his family, Michele and Lucky had spent a magical weekend roaming the dunes, beaches and quaint towns of the tiny peninsula that juts from the coast of Massachusetts into the Atlantic Ocean.

And it was there that Michele had made another promise to Lucky. 'I told her that I would sprinkle her ashes in all of the beautiful places in the world.'

Lucky may have gone, but the next leg of her incredible journey was about to begin.

Lucky's legacy was far reaching. In 2006, a year and a half after her death, Michele was running a sustainability-minded pet store in Boston and online, Lucky Dog Organics, named in honour of her pet. In her spare time, she was also doing one-on-one holistic behavioural dog training. Her world still revolved around dogs, and Lucky was never far from her thoughts, but she still felt she wasn't ready to be a 'dog mum' again just yet.

'Apparently,' she laughs, 'no one told Bella that.'

Michele's neighbours had quickly come to know her as 'the dog lady', so when the owners of a local coffee shop spotted an emaciated boxer puppy in the back of a pick-up truck parked outside the Walgreens pharmacy next door, it was Michele they called. She could tell with just a glance that the dog was malnourished, and asked the owners if they would relinquish the frail dog to her. They agreed and suddenly, despite her best intentions, Michele had a four-legged friend once more. Her name was Bella, and even though she was just skin and bone, Michele could see that the fawn-coloured dog was indeed beautiful.

Just as she had with Lucky, Michele planned to care for Bella for a little while, then find her a loving forever home. And just as with Lucky, fate had other ideas.

'My plan was to nurse her back to vibrancy and then find her a good family, so I home cooked for her, then switched her to a raw diet,' she says. 'I trained her and then, three months after I rescued her, and just as I was about to find her a home, she was stolen from me.'

It was July, and Michele had been at a rehearsal performance of the Boston Pops Orchestra, an offshoot of the Boston Symphony Orchestra that performs classical renditions of pop songs. On her way home, she stopped at the same Walgreens pharmacy she had rescued Bella from months earlier. She tethered Bella to a gate in front of the store for a matter of moments while she ran inside to buy popcorn.

When she returned, Bella was gone.

'Her leash had been unlatched from her harness and unlooped from the gate, and she was taken,' she recalls.

'I knew that I had a very short window of time to get her back, and that the chances were strong that she was still on the street somewhere.'

Instinct took over and Michele began running and screaming with all the gusto she could muster. She yelled again and again that her boxer had been stolen, and implored every single person she passed to join her in her search. She dialled 911, and asked a passing taxi driver to radio his dispatcher, who in turn broadcast Bella's description to all other taxis in the vicinity. Michele called her friends with the news, and they immediately set to work creating 'lost dog' posts to share on Facebook, Twitter and the online classifieds site Craigslist.

Two police officers arrived on the scene and offered to drive Michele around the area in their cruiser. But as the minutes ticked agonisingly by, there was no sign of Bella. Michele couldn't believe it. How could she have vanished in such a short space of time? Surely somebody had seen *something*. And amid her panic, Michele was also nagged by guilt. She had rescued Bella from a clearly terrible situation and given her a second chance, yet still mired in grief for Lucky, she had been planning to give her away. In that moment, she made a vow. 'In my mind I said, *If I get her back, she's staying with me*,' she recalls.

An instant later, a man walking his dog flagged down the police car. Michele had already spoken to him before teaming up with the police officers.

'He was standing in front of an apartment building and said he had seen a woman taking Bella inside,' she says.

Her heart pounded like a kick drum as the officers ventured into the building. Once inside, they heard the unmistakable sound of a dog whimpering from behind a closed apartment door. They went to that apartment and discovered Bella inside with an extremely intoxicated woman. She told the police she was simply 'taking the dog for a walk'. The woman was later charged with drug offences, but never prosecuted for stealing Bella.

'When the police walked out of that building with Bella, she nearly leapt into my arms,' says Michele. True to her vow, any thoughts of finding Bella a new home were instantly forgotten. Whatever lay ahead of them now, it was a journey they would make side by side. 'We were a team from there on out.'

Bella, as Michele quickly discovered, was Lucky's polar opposite. Now fully restored to good health, and instinctively understanding that Michele was her human for life, Bella seemed to decide it was time to let her personality shine through in all its technicolour glory.

'She just woke up loving life every day. She would sometimes wake me up with her little nub tail wagging – that was how excited she was to face the day. She was a spitfire, ever curious, bratty and challenging, but incredibly loving.'

And while Lucky had been an old soul who had much to teach Michele about life, Bella needed and appreciated her mistress's guiding hand. 'Bella was very much looking to me to guide her. She also reminded me not to take everything so seriously,' she says. 'Bella was like a child in so many ways, whereas with Lucky I sometimes felt like she was my mentor.'

Bella also became Michele's travel companion as she embarked on Lucky's posthumous journey to all the beautiful places she had promised to show her. Together, they scattered Lucky's ashes all across the US, from the lovely, quiet backyard of a mid-century house in the Seattle suburb of Bellevue to Florida's St Petersburg beach. Bella and Michele also accompanied Lucky to Vermont's Lake Pauline, the dog parks of Manhattan, Denver's Cheesman Park, where she loved to play fetch, the beach at Cape Elizabeth in Maine, the banks of Boston's Charles River, the woods in Hadley, Massachusetts, and the Arnold Arboretum in the Boston suburb of Jamaica Plain, 'home to many bunny chases through the rose bushes'.

On the first anniversary of Lucky's death, Michele also returned to Cape Cod, this time with Bella in tow. But when the time came to scatter Lucky's ashes there, Michele made that part of the journey alone.

'I stood in a white-out blizzard at the end of the Cape and sprinkled her into the ocean, just me and some seagulls that were also stupid enough to be out in such conditions,' she says.

Bella had a thirst for adventure and never tired of her cross-country travels with Michele. Her natural lust for life made it all the more obvious that, on 4 December 2011, something was very wrong. When she awoke that morning she was slow, quiet, and unresponsive. She dozed all day, and around noon Michele decided to curl up next to her for a nap.

'I reached for her paw, as I often did when we slept, and I thought it was colder than it should be. So I reached for the other one, which was tucked under her, and it was even colder,' she says. 'My next instinct was to look at her gums. When I saw that they were white, I knew that she needed to go to the vet immediately.'

After five years of Bella's 24/7 joy and exuberance, Michele was worried by this sudden turn; pale gums can be a sign of low blood pressure, low body temperature, or internal bleeding. But she knew that her beloved boxer was strong in both body and spirit. Whatever was making Bella unwell, Michele was certain she would conquer it.

'I thought that because Bella was healthier than Lucky was, and younger, she would have more time. We would find the tumour or we would stop whatever bleed was happening, and we would kick its ass,' she says. 'I felt that this was why I was working so hard to make her so incredibly healthy – so that if anything like this happened she would be prepared to take it down.'

Michele's veterinarian quickly determined that internal bleeding was indeed the cause of Bella's lethargy and pale gums. They tried everything, gave Bella multiple blood transfusions, but they just couldn't stanch the bleeding. Late that Sunday night, the vet delivered the terrible news: nothing more could be done for Bella.

Michele understood that it was her responsibility to end Bella's suffering. It was up to her to free her loyal, goofy companion from pain, to help her gently slip away. Devastatingly, Bella understood too.

'Until a few minutes before she died, she didn't know what was going on. When I finally realised what I needed to do, when I looked at her and she saw it in my eyes, she let out a scream that to this day just brings tears to my eyes,' she says. 'She wanted to know why, and I couldn't answer her.'

Bella passed away in Michele's arms shortly after midnight. The cause of her internal bleeding was never conclusively established, but its location in her belly led vets to suspect it was an aggressive tumour on her liver or spleen.

The next day, Michele made a sad tour of her Boston neighbourhood, sharing the news of Bella's death with the community that had made them feel so welcome.

'I walked our walk and I delivered her photo, with a note thanking people personally, to every coffee shop, store, and neighbour that was a part of our routine,' she says. 'I knew that if I hid away I would face a harder struggle later as everyone asked where Bella was. It was easier to deliver the news right away, and so I went to every place and cried a lot and got lots of hugs. Her picture is still up in some of those places. She was a little bit like the mayor of our neighbourhood.'

With Bella joining Lucky in the great dog park in the sky, Michele was bereft, but redoubled her efforts to send both of her girls on a bittersweet world tour. As well as all the stunning locations where she now rests in the US, Lucky had also 'visited' beaches in Melbourne and Brisbane, the streets of Paris, a sheep field in Kent, England, and a mountain-top overlooking a small village in Nepal. Her ashes had even been swept away on a fragrant breeze from the top of the Eiffel Tower.

'It made sense that Bella would become part of the journey too,' says Michele. 'The only locations I really chose were related to bringing Lucky back to Denver, to Brooklyn and to Cape Cod. The rest of the locations were related to friends' travels. I would ask people, and if they said yes, Lucky – and now Bella – would go along.'

Bella has since joined Lucky at Cape Cod, several locations in New York and Massachusetts, and at the dog beach at Del Mar in California. The girls' ashes have also been scattered together in India, the Caribbean island of St Barts, and at a lookout above Manly on Sydney's Northern Beaches. It seems strange that the dogs were never together in life, but fitting that in death they are united by Michele's devotion to them.

'I didn't have a geographical limitation to my plan. It felt natural to just spread out as far as I was able,' Michele says. 'They were lovely, adventurous girls, and they have travelled a far greater deal than I have, even though it has been posthumously.'

While Michele admits some who learn about her commitment to Lucky and Bella's journey 'think I am nuts', she says she's been touched by most people's willingness to help her facilitate her dogs' expedition. In fact, she says the responses she receives to her 'kooky' request – 'Hey, can you spread my dead dogs' ashes for me on your trip?' – is a handy way to get a sense of someone's character.

'There was a man I dated for a few years, and shortly after we started dating I asked him to spread Lucky for me during a trip he was making to Europe. It was early days, but he didn't judge and I believe that was one of the many reasons I fell so deeply in love with him. It is a strange request from some girl you just started dating, kind of kooky,' she says. 'He jumped a fence and spread her in that sheep field in England, and also scattered her in Melbourne during a summer storm. It was a very selfless act on his part, and showed me who he was.'

But whether her friends and family understand her bond with Lucky and Bella, whether they think her decision to act as a sort of spiritual travel agent for her erstwhile pets is odd, Michele is unapologetic.

'I just shrug,' she says. 'To be honest, I've had a very intense relationship with the dogs in my life, and I think it is better to be considered a fool for loving a dog too deeply than to be the fool who missed out on the experience of that type of unconditional love because they only saw a dog.'

She doesn't see an end to Lucky and Bella's globetrotting, and when the time comes, she intends to join them in their roaming. 'I still have a significant bit of them left, and when it is a very small amount then they will wait for me to join them and people will be instructed what to do next,' she explains. 'My own end of life plan is to be mixed together with the ashes of all my dogs, and spread together around the world.'

Geographically speaking, this has been Lucky and Bella's posthumous journey – but it has been a spiritual journey for Michele, too. It is a quest that has moved everyone who has been a part of it.

'I'm a fairly spiritual person in general. I think to start this adventure, one would need to be. And I do think it's helped others who have participated. I've been told that sharing in this process has been very powerful and meaningful for those who have been involved,' she says.

Time has dulled the sadness of losing Lucky and Bella, and being able to fulfill her promise to her girls is a great comfort to Michele. But she knows the pain of their loss will never truly leave her, and this journey has helped her to make peace with that knowledge.

'Grief is a process that is never truly final. It evolves and grows with you,' she says. 'I will never forget or truly get over it, but that actually makes me happy. I have paw-shaped scars on my heart, and I have lived because I have loved.'

Lucky, Bella and Michele shared a rich and joyful life together, and though they are parted temporarily, they are the fortunate ones; the ones who know that death is not the end, but simply the beginning of another journey.

SLUM DOG EXTRAORDINAIRE

DINAH'S STORY

The dog would have to go. With an exasperated sigh, Jamila rolled over and switched on the bedside lamp. The black and white mutt stood in the doorway, batting her long eyelashes as light filled the room. She stared intently at Jamila, silent for a brief, wonderful moment. Her tail whipped back and forth like an antenna in a stiff breeze.

Then she started barking again, even louder and more insistently than before. Jamila groaned. She couldn't understand how such a tiny dog could yap at such volume, and for so long, apparently without even drawing breath. She hoped her neighbours were heavy sleepers; the puppy had been barking for what felt like hours, though it was probably no more than ten minutes. Still, this much noise at such an uncivilised hour was definitely pushing the friendship.

'I'm not going to play with you. Go downstairs and go to sleep!' Jamila hissed. 'Do you want to be sent back to Morocco?' She spoke in a melange of French and Moroccan Arabic. The dog had only been in the Netherlands a couple of weeks; it was unlikely she would respond to commands in Dutch. She didn't exactly seem flush in the brains department, after all.

But miraculously, the puppy turned and disappeared from the doorway. Jamila heard her little paws skittering down the staircase. Heaving a sigh of relief, she flipped off the light and sank back into the pillows. The dog would have to go, she thought again. She couldn't have her sleep disrupted on top of having to walk and feed and entertain the creature every day. She hadn't even wanted a dog in the first place. She had far too much on her plate with her busy job at the theatre and her frenetic social life. Her sister would simply have to find somewhere else for her pet to live.

Sleep was pulling at the edges of her consciousness when the barking started again. The racket amplified as the puppy raced up the stairs and was a bona fide cacophony by the time she burst into the bedroom once more. Jamila switched on the lamp again.

'What? What is it, you stupid dog?!'

The puppy spun in circles, without so much as a pause in her bellowing. She may have been a novice dog owner, but Jamila had read enough training books to know that this sort of attention-seeking behaviour had to be nipped in the bud. She leaned over and gave the dog a light spank on her rump. This din couldn't go on – Jamila had to let the puppy know who was boss.

The dog stilled momentarily, just long enough to fix Jamila with a glare of pure affront. Then, with a nimble leap that belied her small size, she sprang onto the bed and gripped the quilt between her teeth. Jamila watched, stunned, as the puppy dragged the covers off the bed, only interrupting her efforts to direct another volley of yips at her.

Suddenly, a chill unfurled at the base of Jamila's spine and crawled all the way up to her neck. Though she was half asleep, instinct told her this wasn't just irksome frolicking in the dead of night; the dog was trying to tell her something.

'Okay,' she said, swinging her legs from the warm cocoon of her bed. 'Okay, you've got my attention. What is it?'

This time, when the dog skipped lightly to the floor and raced out of the room, Jamila was hot on her heels. They sped down the Rotterdam townhouse's old wooden staircase in tandem.

Jamila smelled the blaze before she saw it. The downstairs living area was filled with acrid smoke that choked her and made her eyes sting. It was several disorienting moments before she could see well enough to determine the source of the pungent fog.

Her kitchen was on fire.

Flames singed the cabinets and licked the ceiling. It was a whisker away from being an inferno – and the brave, determined little puppy had been trying to warn her for the past five minutes. The same puppy Jamila had been planning to evict just seconds ago.

She grabbed the dog, called the fire brigade and dashed outside. As she stood in the darkness, listening to the wail of approaching sirens, Jamila shivered – whether from cold or shock, she couldn't tell. The puppy was quiet now; she had achieved her mission and her relief was palpable.

Jamila hugged the dog close to her chest. 'Okay,' she whispered into one velvety soft ear. 'I understand now why you're here.'

This dog wasn't going anywhere.

The year was 1998. Jamila El Maroudi was 'not a dog person at all'. Dogs represented responsibility and routine. She had wanderlust in her blood, and pets forced people to stay in one place. Then aged in her twenties, Jamila was having too much fun, and had too much of the world left to explore, to saddle herself with such a burden.

Born in Morocco, Jamila emigrated to Rotterdam in the Netherlands when she was three. But her parents kept a house in the Moroccan capital, Rabat, and made the trip back to their homeland often to see friends and extended family there. When Jamila's sister, Hasna, reached high school, the girls' mother promised her a pet dog as a reward for earning good grades. The catch was that the dog would stay in Morocco, where it would be looked after by Jamila's aunt Zmeia while the family was back in Rotterdam. Hasna agreed; she most definitely *was* a dog person, and a pet dog was a pet dog, regardless of its address.

Privately, Jamila thought the bargain a bit harebrained, but she was backpacking through Israel at the time and didn't feel it was her place to weigh in.

'It was silly because they only went to Rabat for holidays, but the house there was much bigger than my parents' home in Holland, so they thought it made more sense to keep the dog there,' says Jamila.

Generally speaking, says Jamila, it is unusual for Muslims to keep pet dogs, although it's not explicitly prohibited in the Quran. In predominantly Muslim Morocco, however, dog ownership is quite common. Aunt Zmeia was tasked with finding a four-legged friend for Hasna. She asked an acquaintance for help, and he said puppies were in plentiful supply in Douar Kharga, one of Rabat's underprivileged, or 'slum', districts.

Zmeia's contact took her to see a tiny black and white female puppy, just a few months old. She knew right away that her niece would fall in love with the pup.

'Not being very savvy, she said, "Tell me how much the dog costs." They thought she had a lot of money, coming into the slums asking questions like that, so they said, "Seven hundred dirham [about A$100],"' Jamila recalls. 'She said, "Okay" and took the dog home.'

Jamila's parents arrived for a visit soon afterwards and, as predicted, Hasna was immediately besotted with her new pet. The only thing she didn't like about the puppy was her name: Rosa.

'Morocco is obsessed with South American soap operas. They're all dubbed in Arabic or French, and every heroine is called Rosa,' Jamila explains. This dog definitely wasn't a Rosa.

The entire El Maroudi family are jazz devotees, so Hasna named the little dog Dinah after American jazz singer and self-proclaimed 'Queen of the Blues' Dinah Washington. It was a fitting choice: one of Washington's biggest hits is the oft-covered 'Unforgettable', and little Dinah would soon prove herself to be that. The Hebrew name also means 'vindicated', and that would ultimately prove fitting as well.

The rules of Dinah's membership of the family were well established: she would remain in Morocco when the family returned to the Netherlands. But Hasna became so attached to her canine companion that, as her two-week holiday came to an end, she couldn't bear to leave her pet behind. After much wheedling, she convinced her parents to allow her to bring Dinah back to Rotterdam. That was as far as they were prepared to relent, however; they were still adamant the puppy would have to be housed elsewhere once they got home.

Hasna wasn't worried about that. She knew of a certain big sister she was sure she could cajole into taking pity on a small, fluffy immigrant.

Then came the next problem: getting the dog back to the Netherlands. The Strait of Gibraltar, Spain, France and

Belgium stood between Dinah and her new home. It didn't look like much on a map – the 3000 kilometre journey could be made by ferry and road, or a five-hour flight – but the reality was more complex.

By law, Dinah required a number of health checks and vaccinations before she could be deemed fit to travel to the Netherlands. The most crucial of these was a rabies vaccine – rabies is endemic in Morocco. The Netherlands requires that dogs are inoculated against rabies at least three weeks before arriving in the country, and demands veterinarian-certified proof of the date of vaccination.

The problem was the El Maroudis were due to fly home in just a week's time.

'They just thought, *We'll get her vaccinated and give the vet a bit of extra money to change the dates on the certificate*, and he did,' says Jamila. 'They bribed the vet.'

On their return to Rotterdam, Hasna immediately pleaded Dinah's case to Jamila, who was twelve years older than her and newly arrived home from her journey through Israel.

'I was not a dog person at all, but I said, "Bring the dog over and I'll see what I can do,"' she says.

First impressions were not positive. Dinah had spent her formative months living a life of wild abandon in the slums of Rabat, and then two weeks having her every whim indulged by Jamila's enraptured sister. She'd had no formal training, nor any informal training for that matter. To say she lacked manners was putting it mildly.

'She was a terrible nutcase of a dog. Really wild. She came into my house and just ran and jumped on couches and tables,' says Jamila. 'She had been hanging around with the kids in the slums. My first thought was, *What am I supposed to do with this thing?*'

With great reluctance, Jamila set about trying to mould the recalcitrant mutt into something vaguely approaching an acceptable housemate. She read books about behaviour and training. She exercised the little dog daily in an effort to burn off some of her boundless energy, which was a chore Jamila felt she could do without. Dinah was an inside dog, and that meant Jamila was forced to escort her outside frequently during the long, bitterly cold European winters for toilet breaks.

Dinah wouldn't even eat dog food. In the slums her owner had fed her aromatic meat tagines, and her gourmand's palate meant she turned up her nose at anything that wasn't homemade.

Nothing seemed to work. Later on Jamila would realise Dinah's exuberance was just typical puppy behaviour. At the time, however, she thought the dog was simply out of control. Two weeks into their awkward relationship, Jamila was at the end of her tether. Dinah had worn out her welcome. Hasna was going to have to make other arrangements.

Then the kitchen caught fire, and just as her name predicted, Dinah was vindicated.

She never discovered the cause of the fire, but that night was a watershed for Jamila and Dinah. From that moment onwards, the pair were inseparable. Though Dinah continued to be thought of as a family dog – and Jamila's sister made regular visits – any questions about the little dog's ongoing custody were emphatically answered.

Jamila worked in marketing for Rotterdamse Schouwburg, one of the Netherlands' leading theatres. She held the position for seven years, and Dinah came to work with her every day.

'We did big productions and had lots of international visitors. We trained her there and she became part of the furniture,' she says. 'She had her own "in" and "out" signs so people would know if she was there or not. She would always be cuddled and patted by everyone. Everybody knew Dinah, but not everybody knew me. People would see me and say, "I didn't recognise you without your dog!"'

Dinah felt so at home at the theatre that she learned to navigate the building by herself. She would take the elevator, often on her own, to the staff cafeteria on the first floor, where she had only to flash her big brown eyes to receive a generous helping of whatever was on the menu that day.

'Once we had a company visiting from Japan and there were forty women all dressed up in kimonos. Before they went on stage they would have dinner in the restaurant,' says Jamila. 'It was like Dinah smelled forty women eating – she just took off downstairs. I followed her, and there were all these women jumping around and clapping their hands in excitement at the sight of her.'

Already a well-travelled dog, Dinah racked up even more air miles as Jamila's companion. In the years after her move to the Netherlands, Dinah twice revisited her old stomping ground in Morocco – and on both occasions seemed eager to show she'd left her inauspicious beginnings behind her.

'Once I said, "Let's go and check out your old 'hood." My sister and I took her down to the slums and it was like she understood where she was,' Jamila says. 'She's got this walk like, "I'm not from here, ladies – I've moved up in the world." She was so arrogant!' Dinah's swagger led Jamila to dub her 'bourghetto' – a combination of 'bourgeois' and 'ghetto'.

Being back in Rabat was also a waymarker of sorts in Jamila and Dinah's spiritual journey together. From her initial ambivalence towards dogs, Jamila's bond with her canine companion meant she was now an avowed 'dog person'.

'She completely changed me – I'm the biggest sucker for dogs now,' she laughs. 'I'd rented a house in Morocco and I would buy dog food and feed the stray dogs around the property. Dinah would come running out and chase them all away, barking at me like, "What are you doing? That's *my* food!"'

For her part, the innate protective instinct that had emerged the night of the kitchen fire was able to flourish in Rabat. The people who lived next door to Jamila's parents had four big German shepherds; at more than 30 kilograms each, they dwarfed 7-kilogram Dinah.

'She used to go outside and play with all the neighbourhood kids in the front yard. One day, one of the shepherds tried to attack one of the children and Dinah just went berserk and chased it away,' Jamila says. 'She's a tiny, tiny mutt, but she put it in its place. To this day, every time she sees a German shepherd, she goes nuts.'

If Jamila was proud of her feisty friend then, she was about to get even prouder.

It was late, but Jamila couldn't sleep. There was something in the air, some portent of danger. She couldn't put her finger on it, but Jamila couldn't deny she felt uneasy in her old townhouse that night.

She took Dinah and her quilt, and went downstairs. She checked that all the windows and doors were locked, then curled up on the sofa. She felt safer down there somehow, with her little dog at her feet. Finally, she drifted into a fitful sleep.

A series of frenzied barks from Dinah yanked her back to consciousness some time later. How long had she been dozing? It could have been minutes, or hours. She was disoriented and couldn't tell for sure.

Fire! Jamila's first thought was one of panic as she scanned the downstairs living area. But unlike the last time Dinah's barking had dragged her from sleep, this time everything looked as it should.

Still, she couldn't shake the jittery feeling that had driven her from her bed, and Dinah's frantic barking did nothing to allay her fear. 'Dinah has always had this really amazing bark, and at that moment it was even more rough than ever. She was just furious,' Jamila recalls.

Dinah raced to the big picture-window that looked out into the garden. In the daytime it flooded the living area with light. Now it was screened by curtains, with just a sliver of glass visible between the bottom of the drapes and the floor. The little dog wiggled into the gap and continued her vociferous attack on whatever was on the other side of the glass.

'If you were outside in the garden lying on your belly, you could see under the curtains. You would be able to see me lying on the couch,' she says. 'Dinah got under the curtains and started going crazy.'

Jamila knew something was out there; the night of the fire had taught her that Dinah didn't behave like this without very good reason. She got up from the sofa and pulled back the curtains.

There, with just a few centimetres of glass between them, was a hulking man performing a lewd act. He was staring at Jamila as he tried to break in through the window.

Although the sight was terrifying, Jamila wasn't scared – just angry. In fact, she was incandescent with rage. She ran outside and – lucky for him – her would-be attacker ran too.

'I wasn't afraid then. Your natural instinct kicks in and you just think, *I need to protect myself*. The dog was going crazy. I was going crazy. I would have attacked him,' she says. 'After I got outside and got the police there, that's when I started shaking and crying.'

The following day, Jamila went to the police station to make a formal statement. It was then that she learned the man was believed responsible for more than a dozen sexual assaults in the area. He had apparently identified Jamila as his next victim. 'The police told me he targeted women who he knew lived alone,' she says. She doesn't believe the man was ever caught.

Dinah had saved Jamila once again. If she needed further proof that the little dog had chosen her, this was it.

'I know that, as small as she was, Dinah would have protected me. After the fire, and then this, that was it for me,' she says. 'This dog was supposed to be with me and protect me, and I will always protect her.'

Jamila and Dinah moved out of the townhouse immediately, and it wasn't long before they would make another incredible journey together.

In 2004, Jamila met a handsome Australian called David. After a whirlwind romance, they got engaged, and then decided to move 16 500 kilometres away to David's hometown, Melbourne.

'The one thing I said had to happen was that Dinah had to come. There was no way I was going anywhere without the dog,' says Jamila. 'Before I met my husband my sister used to say, "The longest relationship you've ever had is with your dog." David and I married in 2006, but Dinah still has my last name.'

This time there would be no fudging of the vaccination records. Australia's quarantine requirements are strict and uncompromising, and there was no getting around the fact that Dinah, by now around seven years old, would have to spend a month in quarantine upon arrival.

As is her easygoing way, Dinah handled the journey with typical self-assurance. For a dog whose journey had taken her from the slums of Morocco to high culture in the Netherlands, a jaunt to the other side of the planet was just one more grand adventure.

It was Jamila who struggled most with her spirited companion's expedition. 'Quarantine was horrible. It was like a dog asylum. She only had to go for four weeks, but it was still too long,' she says. 'When she came out she couldn't bark anymore because she'd barked so much she was hoarse. I would never do that again to a dog.'

More than a decade after her second emigration, Dinah is now a sprightly eighteen-year-old – but she still can't speak the language. 'People ask me, "Does she speak Australian?" but she doesn't. The only English word she responds to is Schmacko,' says Jamila.

Dinah is deaf now, and struggles to jump onto the sofa or bed with the same ease as in her younger days. 'But she's still a very happy dog,' says Jamila.

And as ever, she is her mistress's unwavering companion. 'I think if I didn't have her here in Australia, I would have been very lonely, especially in the first year,' she says. 'She is still considered a family dog. My sisters will say to me, "I'm coming to Australia, not to see you but to see Dinah." But she is more my dog than anyone else's.'

In 2015, elderly Dinah had a seizure. She woke Jamila at four o'clock in the morning, but where previously she had heroically saved Jamila's life, now she needed Jamila to save hers.

'Her tongue was hanging out and her eyes were really weird. She couldn't walk. We thought that was it, that we were going to have to take her to the vet and help her pass,' says Jamila. 'But something in me said, *No, you're not going anywhere.*'

And so she uttered the magic word – 'Schmacko' – and Dinah lifted her head. 'She got up, and within half an hour she was back to normal,' she says.

But the episode was a harsh reminder that, sadly, dogs don't live forever – as the American author Agnes Sligh Turnbull once quipped, it's their only flaw. Knowing that Dinah is approaching the end of her extraordinary life has made Jamila all the more grateful for the journey they have shared.

'I never could have imagined what she would come to mean to me. I never even wanted her. I was in my twenties when she came into my life and I just thought *This is too much hassle,*' she says. 'Now I'm in my forties and I would do anything for her. We're a duo.'

From slum dog to beloved pet, from Morocco to the Netherlands to Melbourne, little Dinah is proof that loving and being loved is the most incredible journey of all.

THE AMAZING RACE

THE IDITAROD STORY

The Shaktoolik checkpoint looked like a war zone. As his team of twelve Alaskan huskies charged into the tiny village on the eastern shore of Norton Sound, the icy Arctic wind buffeting them from all sides, Christian Turner was shocked to see defeat on the faces of the mushers who had arrived ahead of him. Of the six that had made it to 'Shak' during a fierce coastal storm the night before, five were still here recuperating. Their dogs were 'parked' haphazardly, as though they had simply refused to take another step. One musher had severe frostbite; his head was swathed in bandages.

Christian was doubly glad he'd listened to the race judges at the last checkpoint, Unalakleet, and stayed the night there to wait out the storm. It meant his dogs were well rested, and everyone at Shak commented on his upbeat mood and broad smile – it had been a while since they'd seen one. The 21-year-old Australian had good reason to feel cheerful: his team of rookie two-year-olds had covered the 60-odd kilometres from Unalakleet in a blistering five and a half hours. He'd heard as he made his way to Shaktoolik that storms were causing problems for teams further north, but the weather out of Unalakleet had been beautiful, and the dogs just wanted to run and run.

Little Lava had led the team for nearly 800 kilometres so far – all the way from the town of Nikolai – and was still showing no signs of slowing. The lead dogs were usually the first to tire, since they were bearing the brunt of breaking the trail. But Lava was a canny little thing: she was on heat, and if she'd been back in the pack the lead males would have been constantly stopping and turning, trying to get to her. It would have destroyed momentum, and Christian would have had no option but to drop her off at a check-point. Clever Lava seemed to understand that she either had to stay in the lead or get left behind. If she was angling for the unofficial Most Valuable Player award, she was going about it the right way.

Still, this was the Iditarod – the greatest and most challenging dog sled race on earth – and the 2014 event was proving particularly tough for all competitors, including Christian. There was an unusual lack of snow for March, which threw up a raft of potentially catastrophic obstacles that mushers who had trained all winter in deep powder simply hadn't factored into their race strategies. As he struck out from the Shaktoolik checkpoint after just two hours' rest – virtually unheard of with a team of such young dogs – Christian knew he would have to to keep his wits about him.

The wind was howling as the team, with Lava still proudly in the lead, headed due north towards the town of Koyuk. As had become her trademark, Lava was the only dog in the team whose tail was wagging as they set out. The storm still lingered, but Christian felt he and the dogs could cope with it. The actual distance of this leg was under 80 kilometres, but experienced Iditarod competitors said it felt like double that because it was flat, featureless and deathly dull. More than 60 kilometres of the stretch was on the frozen Norton Sound. Teams stalled there every year because their dogs got spooked by the vast, white expanse of sea ice and either refused to begin the crossing or tried to turn back halfway across.

The late afternoon light was fading rapidly as Christian drove his team out onto the ice. Almost immediately, he could tell that the powerful wind had blown what little snow cover there was out to sea. The trail was delineated with reflective markers, but in the stormy conditions it was hard to see them. Once the sun set completely, it would be almost impossible.

'If you get caught in a storm on the ice,' race organisers warned the mushers each year, 'you will be in very serious trouble.' Christian was about to find out just how serious.

They made reasonable time until the wind really picked up. Suddenly, snow was blowing in sideways and visibility was virtually nil. With no snow covering the ice for the dogs to grip or the sled's brake to snag, the gale pushed the team off the trail – straight towards the open ocean.

'The ice shifts and creates big crevasses and it's very hard to keep in a straight line. It was sharp, sheer ice and the dogs were falling over,' Christian says. 'To my left was open water. I didn't know which way was up. I was very scared then.'

In the pitch dark, all Christian could do was direct the beam of his headlamp towards where he thought the trail was, searching for the flash of a marker. Painstakingly, the team covered the next few miles this way. For all her tenacity, Lava was struggling upfront, the wind full in her face as she strained to spot the markers and steer the team towards them. Christian could see the anxiety in her eyes, so he pulled the team up and walked down the line to her. He gave her a pat and some words of encouragement, and then they ploughed on into the blizzard.

Christian called 'Haw!' and Lava responded, steering the team left and back onto the trail. They inched forward, with Christian stopping repeatedly to walk to the front of his team in search of another marker. They were moving at a crawl, but at least they were moving.

And then . . . nothing. Christian walked to the front again, but couldn't see the next marker. He turned around, but couldn't make out the last one either. He had no idea if his team was even on the trail anymore. They could have been mere footsteps from plunging into the sea. Lava didn't know either; she was weaving from left to right, looking for the route. All Christian could see in any direction was darkness. All he could hear was the shriek of the storm, which was worsening with every passing minute.

The words of his mentor, the dogs' owner Dallas Seavey, echoed through Christian's mind. Dallas always said that if a musher let his team quit once, they were more likely to quit again in subsequent races. A good musher knew his team's limits, Dallas said, and pushed them right to the edge – but never past it. In 2012, aged just twenty-five, Dallas had become the youngest-ever musher to win the Iditarod. He knew what he was talking about, and he was a good friend to Christian – there was no way the Aussie rookie was going to put Dallas's dogs at risk.

All Iditarod competitors are required to carry an Emergency Position Indicating Radio Beacon (EPIRB), and for the first time Christian contemplated using his. To do so would mean he instantly forfeited the race, but he couldn't see any other option but to summon help. At this point, finishing the race was a distant third on his list of priorities. The dogs' safety was his chief concern, closely followed by his own.

But something stopped him. Despite the dangerous conditions, and despite their obvious fatigue, the dogs were still happy. They still wanted to keep going, even though doing so at that moment might have been suicidal. These young dogs had far exceeded Christian's expectations so far, and he knew they had more to give. All they had to do was get through the storm, and get off the ice.

His mind made up, Christian drove his snow hook – the sled's anchor – deep into the ice and flipped the sled to create a barrier against the relentless wind. The temperature was plummeting and the dogs were freezing despite the insulated jackets and booties they each wore. There was no way they would survive a night on the ice without additional protection; the exposure could kill them all.

As quickly as he could manage with his frozen fingers, Christian unloaded the sled. He put the three female huskies into its cargo bed and zipped the sled bag closed, then zipped four males into his sleeping bag. That left five males out in the cold. Christian tethered them together as closely as he could and positioned them behind the sleeping bag, hoping it would act as a windbreak. The dogs huddled together like penguins.

Finally, Christian could focus on his own safety. He was freezing cold and so, so tired. He knew that sleeping on the ice in these ferocious conditions was risky. There was a real possibility hypothermia would set in and he wouldn't wake up. But he had no choice – he simply had to rest. 'It was like sleeping on an ice block,' he says. 'I knew I shouldn't be going to sleep, but I was so exhausted.'

He put on every piece of clothing he had, pulled up his hood and lay down, curling himself around the tight knot of dogs and hoping.

*

In every possible sense, the unforgiving Alaskan wilderness is a hell of a long way from the New South Wales north-coast town of Dorrigo, where Christian was born and spent his early years. And racing teams of huskies across frozen, isolated terrain is about as far removed as it gets from the summertime pursuits he enjoyed as a teenager living on Sydney's Northern Beaches.

But while he 'definitely wasn't a snow person' growing up, Christian became fascinated with the sport of mushing – and its Holy Grail, the Iditarod – virtually the moment he first heard about it.

'I've really loved dogs from when I was young. My dad had a farm in Dorrigo and had farm dogs,' he says. 'Later he lived at Dural, on the outskirts of Sydney, and through going out and spending time with him there I met a lady who was a former agility champion, so I trained in agility with a border collie.'

In 2008, after completing his first year of a communications degree, the then nineteen-year-old deferred his studies to travel in Canada. The plan was to spend the northern winter snowboarding, but his travel funds quickly dried up and Christian decided to look for work.

He applied for a job as a kennel hand with a company that operated dog-sled tours in the spectacular Rocky Mountains. 'I embellished my resume and said I'd done a lot more stuff with dogs than I actually had,' he laughs. 'I hadn't done dog sledding before, and the place they do the tours is just breathtaking. You can't hear any cars. You don't see any people. You're out in the wilderness. It was really mind-blowing.'

His job involved cleaning up after the dogs and taking tourists out on short sledding tours. Though the work wasn't too taxing and the scenery was stunning, after his first winter in the job Christian found himself hankering for a new challenge.

'I started getting a bit bored, and that's when I started getting into racing. I said to the tour operators, "I'll come and work for you again next winter if I can use your dogs to race,"' he says.

They agreed, and the following winter he returned and started entering local races. Mushing – as competitive dog sledding is known – is a hugely popular winter sport in Canada, and it wasn't long before Christian had competed in all the nearby events. He started looking further afield, and after three seasons with the tour company, he'd done virtually all of the sled races in Canada.

'Short distances weren't very challenging, and I started winning. Once you get into that group you realise there're bigger and better races, and most of them are up north,' Christian says.

'North' meant Canada's Northwest Territories, the Yukon, and Alaska, the largest and most sparsely populated US state. Collectively, they are some of the most remote and inhospitable – albeit stunningly beautiful – regions on the planet, which is what makes them ideal for host-ing iconic long-distance dog sled races. These include the

500-kilometre Ivakkak race in northern Quebec; Alaska's 708-kilometre Kobuk 440, which is billed as the toughest dog sled race above the Arctic Circle; and the famed Yukon Quest, which covers 1600 kilometres between Whitehorse, Yukon, and Fairbanks, Alaska, every February.

And then there was the Iditarod Trail Sled Dog Race. Known as 'the last great race on earth', the 1600-kilometre event begins in Anchorage, in south central Alaska, on the first Saturday in March, and ends at Nome, on the western Bering Sea coast, when the last musher crosses the finish line.

The race takes its name from the historic Iditarod Trail, which was constructed by the Federal Government in 1910 to allow dog sled teams to deliver mail and supplies to the settlements that had sprung up across Alaska during the gold rush of the late nineteenth century and were isolated by snow and ice during the long winter months.

In 1925, mushers famously used the trail to deliver medication to Nome, which was in the grip of a diphtheria epidemic. The twenty teams involved made the 1100-kilometre journey in around six days, saving hundreds of lives.

The trail was used less frequently after World War II, and the advent of snowmachines in the 1960s rendered dog sled teams largely obsolete. In 1964, a committee of residents of the towns of Wasilla and Knik came together to brainstorm ideas to mark the forthcoming centenary of Alaska becoming a US territory following its purchase from Russia. Committee chairwoman Dorothy Page proposed a dog sled race over the Iditarod Trail. She joined forces with fellow committee member Joe Redington Sr, who had long been interested in the historically significant trail and hoped the centennial race would help preserve it and bring national recognition.

With teams of volunteers undertaking the backbreaking work of clearing a stretch of the trail, a 90-kilometre race was staged between Knik and the town of Big Lake in the centenary year, 1967. The race was held again in 1969, and then everybody lost interest.

Everybody, that is, but Joe Redington Sr, whose passion for the trail – along with his vision for the race – only grew. As well as his undiminished drive to preserve the trail, he also wanted to save Alaskan huskies and sled dog culture – both of which were in danger of being phased out of existence as the use of snowmachines became ubiquitous.

The first official long-distance Iditarod Trail Sled Dog Race was held in 1973. The winner, Dick Wilmarth, took almost three weeks to reach Nome. The Iditarod Trail has both a northern and a southern section, and in the early years competitors only used the northern route. When organisers realised that smaller villages on the trail were being heavily impacted by the large group of mushers, press and volunteers descending every year, they decided to use both sections of the trail. Today, mushers race the northern route in even-numbered years, while in odd years they head south. The change means that the northern villages of Ruby, Galena and Nulato only have to deal with the race juggernaut every other year, and also that the towns of Shageluk, Anvik and Grayling can participate. Plus, the event now passes through the actual ghost town of Iditarod.

Since 1973, the race has grown every year, and captured the world's imagination. As his passion for mushing grew, Christian knew he had to attempt it.

After working the 2010–11 winter in the Rockies, Christian returned to Australia in early 2011 and started working in the mines at Karratha in the Pilbara region of Western Australia. He was still working there during the northern winter of 2011–12. His aim was simply to make enough money to begin his Iditarod preparations in Alaska, but it was a culture shock to say the least.

'It's a beautiful place, with red rocks and beautiful scenery, but it's just so hot. It was forty degrees-plus all the time and there's flies and red dust,' he says. 'After Canada, it was hard to enjoy it. It felt like jail.'

To distract himself from the heat and tedium, Christian posted an advertisement on an online dog sledding forum in early 2012, seeking a position with a long-distance racing kennel. Several teams responded, including Dallas Seavey, who had just won that year's Iditarod. The year before, Dallas had also won the Yukon Quest in his first attempt, becoming only the second rookie ever to do so. His father, Mitch Seavey, had won the Iditarod in 2004 (and would do so again in 2013 at 53, becoming the oldest musher to take the title), and his grandfather, Dan Seavey, was a veteran musher who had competed in the very first Iditarod in 1973 – and then three more for good measure.

Dallas proposed taking Christian on as a kennel hand. He would live with the Seaveys and look after the dogs, and in return Dallas would train him and help him qualify for the Iditarod, a task that required participation in 1200-kilometres' worth of sanctioned races.

The Seavey family were Iditarod royalty. Accepting Dallas's offer was a no-brainer.

'None of the other mushers who responded were my age, so that was the main decider. I thought, *He's just won the Iditarod, he must know what he's doing*,' Christian says.

He started working with the Seaveys in the northern winter of 2012–13. 'Dallas had never guaranteed me a team in the Iditarod. He just said, "If you work out I can get you qualified in your first season,"' he says. 'Before I'd even qualified he said, "Are you coming back? I'll give you a team next season."'

The most formidable dog sled journey on earth was within his reach.

The storm was still raging when Christian awoke three or four hours after going to sleep on the frozen Norton Sound but, mercifully, conditions looked to be calming. The horizontal snow had stopped and the wind seemed less brutal. It was still oppressively dark though and he couldn't see a trail marker anywhere.

As the dogs woke and stretched around him, Christian ventured as far away from his makeshift camp as he dared. At last, he spotted a reflective glimmer in the distance. He lined the team up, indefatigable Lava in the lead once more, and slowly they set off, creeping from marker to marker. As the weather eased further and visibility improved, Christian found he could now see two, three markers ahead of the team, and they were finally able to pick up their pace.

They were back in business.

Christian was glad he'd been able to ride out the storm. After all the training he had done, all the hard graft he'd put in just to get to the Iditarod start line, he would have been devastated if he'd had to pull out of the race. By trusting him to take his 'puppy team' – as the two-year-old canine competitors are known – through the race, Dallas had shown he had faith in Christian. He was determined to prove it was justified.

'More than 50 per cent of the race is figuring out what your dogs can and can't do,' he says.

It's common practice for the big racing kennels to bring in other mushers to put their novice dogs through their paces in events like the Iditarod, while the experienced mushers compete with their older, race-seasoned canines. Dallas Seavey has more than 100 Alaskan huskies, while Mitch has over 240, so there are plenty of young dogs that need to be shown the ropes each racing season (the family also runs a sled tour business).

'In their first year they'll do 2400 kilometres, just training – no racing. In year two, if the kennel has the money and the mushers, they might do a big race like the Yukon Quest or the Iditarod,' Christian says. 'If you don't do that your younger team is totally inexperienced when you're trying to run them.'

Serious training for the Iditarod starts in the northern Autumn, when there's little or no snow on the ground and the dogs run on dirt tracks. By the time winter descends and the snow starts falling in earnest, the teams are running 65 kilometres a day – or sometimes twice a day, with a four-hour rest in between. Then it's on to overnight training runs.

'I started to take the cold in my stride, which is probably why I just kept going back to Canada every year,' Christian says. 'But sometimes you're out there at four o'clock in the morning and it's −40 °C and that's when you're like, *What am I doing?* You can feel very isolated and alone.'

Christian helped Dallas maintain detailed spreadsheets for every single one of his dogs, recording data such as whether it had been injured and how many miles it had run over the season and in its lifetime. 'It's not just going out and playing in the snow,' he says. 'When the big money gets involved that's when people get very serious.' The Iditarod purse of at least US$750 000 is split between the top thirty mushers. The winner also receives a new car.

But while the dogs are a valuable commodity, mushers also develop close bonds with their canine team. Some of the dogs Christian took through the Iditarod in 2014 he had actually helped bring into the world during his first season working with Dallas.

'You definitely bond with each dog individually. I fed some of those dogs as eight-week-old puppies. I trained them to wear a racing harness. They look to you for support and if you ever let them down they remember it,' he says. 'The Seavey dogs are very determined and stoic. They know they have a job to do, and when it's go time it's go time. They're sort of like a military unit.'

As his dogs bounded into the Koyuk checkpoint after their hellish night on Norton Sound, Christian couldn't have been prouder of them. They were greeted by a group of worried mushers and volunteers who had been watching Christian's gruelling struggle across the sea ice via GPS and were on the verge of sending out a search party.

Their concern was understandable: the near-catastrophe on Norton Sound wasn't Christian's first serious trial in that year's race. Plus, he was already down to twelve dogs, having left four tired team members at checkpoints along the way. (All competitors must start the Iditarod in Anchorage with sixteen dogs and finish with at least six; fatigued or injured dogs may be left at checkpoints, where they can receive veterinary care and be safely transported to the finish line.)

His first big test had come about 400 kilometres into the race, between the villages of Rohn and Nikolai, on a 65-kilometre stretch of trail called the Farewell Burn. To mushers it is simply 'The Burn'. It was the site of the largest forest fire in Alaska's history, with more than a million and a half acres razed in the summer of 1978. The trail through The Burn was virtually impassable for years after the fire before it was cleared by the government. Now the eerie burnt-out woodland doesn't pose much of a problem, except in years of low snow – years just like 2014.

Christian had felt buoyant as he entered The Burn. The dogs were running beautifully and he was on track for an impressive overall time. 'I thought I was going to be in the top twenty and win Rookie of the Year,' he says.

But the lack of snow meant that, instead of gliding through The Burn, Christian had to negotiate a rough, rocky trail peppered with exposed tree stumps. Steering was tough, and controlling his speed was difficult because there was no snow for the sled's brake to grab onto.

'A stump went right under the sled and broke the brake off. I got faster and faster and hit a tree coming around a corner, and the gangline snapped,' he says.

The gangline is the central cable that tethers the dogs to the sled; their individual harnesses are then tethered to the gangline via shorter tug lines. The dogs are also lashed together in pairs with neck lines. Sled dogs are trained to slow when they feel pressure on the gangline, and to speed up when that pressure eases. If the gangline goes completely slack, they will run as fast as their legs can carry them.

Sure enough, fouteen of Christian's sixteen dogs had raced off into the distance, leaving him and the two 'wheel dogs' immediately in front of the sled in their dust. That the gangline had snapped ahead of the wheel dogs was one small mercy – the force of fourteen dogs pulling on two dogs' neck line could have broken their necks.

'I quickly checked on the two on my sled and then I took off after the other dogs. I found them 3 or 4 kilometres down the road, tangled in a big branch,' he says. 'They were all biting each other. It didn't help that I had females on heat, so the boys were fighting over the girls.'

It was frustrating, but he'd reminded himself it could have been much worse. 'If you have a loose cable a dog can fall over and can't get back up because the other dogs just keep pulling, so they just get dragged to death,' he says. 'Or one of the dogs can step in a hole and break its leg. We were lucky that didn't happen.'

He separated the males from the females and tied them up as best he could with what he had. Then he trudged the 4 kilometres back to his sled and the wheel dogs. The two dogs couldn't pull Christian and the fully laden sled on their own, and it was too heavy for him to pull by hand. He had no choice but to unload it, leave all his gear on the side of the trail, and then walk the sled and the dogs to the rest of the team. He then made two more trips to bring his gear back to the sled.

'The whole thing took me twelve hours. I wasn't even thinking about finishing the race by then, just getting my dogs together in one place and fed,' he says. 'I was totally dehydrated because I was wearing all this snow gear, and I'd completely run out of water and couldn't melt any snow because there wasn't any. It was getting pretty dire.'

While the dogs slept, Christian got to work repairing the sled. He put on a new brake and changed the runners underneath; the ones he'd started with had been ground to dust by the rough terrain. He replaced the broken section of gangline with a piece of rope. By the time he'd finished, he had been overtaken by every other team in the race and was in last place.

But at least he was still *in* the race, and if that was the worst thing that happened over the next 1200 kilometres, he'd be doing well.

Then, of course, came Norton Sound. His struggle through The Burn felt like a holiday in comparison.

Despite the scare out on the sea ice, Christian's team was in surprisingly good shape when they finally reached Koyuk. He'd made up some of the ground he'd lost at The Burn, and he knew he had a chance now to make up even more. After a short break, and bidding farewell to a dog called Maui who was too tired to continue, Christian and his eleven remaining dogs began the final 275-kilometre push to Nome.

Christian finished the 2014 race, his maiden Iditarod journey, in eleven days, four hours, fifty-two minutes and thirty seconds. He was thirty-eighth of forty-nine finishers in what was one of the toughest Iditarods in memory. There were multiple injuries to both dogs and humans, some serious, and twenty mushers withdrew or were scratched, including veteran Jeff King. Dallas Seavey won the race in a time of eight days and thirteen minutes. His father, Mitch, was third.

It had been a steep learning curve for Christian. The first thing he did after crossing the finish line was give Lava a huge hug. 'The best moment for me was watching Lava lead constantly and really excel,' he says. 'It didn't matter what I put her through, or what the race threw at her, she was just constantly impressing. She's a great little dog.'

Though he was happy simply to have completed the iconic Iditarod, Christian felt he had unfinished business with the last great race on earth. 'I thought I was so well versed in what to expect, but then there was no snow. I would have done a lot better if I hadn't had the obstacles I did.'

When he returned for his second attempt, in 2015, he felt confident. He had an older, stronger, more experienced team of Seavey dogs, and there was plenty of snow on the ground. And after the previous year, he felt he could handle anything the Iditarod could throw at him.

He was right. Christian finished the 2015 event in nine days and sixteen hours, claiming fifteenth place. He won US$20 000 for his trouble. It was the fastest time for a competitor from the southern hemisphere, and he was just two hours out of the top ten. 'There were three teams in front of me and I just couldn't catch them,' he says. 'But I felt like I was walking on air. After 2014 it felt like a walk in the park. It was a completely different race. It snowed the whole time and I just had so much fun.'

It was an auspicious year for the Seavey kennel. As well as Christian's top-twenty finish, Dallas won the race – running many of the dogs broken in by Christian the year before – and Mitch came second.

Dallas Seavey won the Iditarod for the fourth time in five years in 2016, finishing with just six dogs in eight days and eleven hours and breaking the speed record he had set in 2014. Continuing the family tradition, Mitch finished second.

Christian didn't compete in 2016. After maintaining a long-distance relationship with his journalist partner, Sarah, for three years, he felt the time had come to return to Australia on a more permanent basis. He now lives in the Northern Rivers region of New South Wales and works as a carpenter.

But he hasn't given up on completing the toughest, most exhilarating dog sled journey on the planet again.

'I'd love to do it again. Dallas is a good friend and the Seaveys have got the best dogs in the world. To come second to Dallas would be pretty cool,' says Christian.

'Being out in nature and working with a natural form of transport is really cool. If you're out there at night you see the northern lights. You don't hear any engine noise. There's no pollution. You're going to places that are otherwise inaccessible and fending for yourself. I think I can tackle any dog sled race now.'

A CHRISTMAS MIRACLE

INKA'S STORY

As first dates go, it was the ideal outing for a pair of dog lovers: a walk on a pristine Gold Coast beach with their respective canine companions. But as Peter Pignolet watched his border collie–shepherd cross, Chai, romp on the white sand with Janneke Geursen's Tasmanian Smithfield, Barney, he couldn't help but feel a twinge of sadness. Something weighed heavily on him, just as it had every day for the past eight years.

Inka should have been there too.

Peter had been working as a chef in the resort town of Airlie Beach, on Queensland's Whitsunday Coast, when he decided in 2000, at the age of thirty-one, the time had come to have a dog of his very own. His neighbour's lovely bitser was expecting, and Peter put in a request for a male puppy.

'I've always liked dogs, and always had family dogs, but it was a big step for me to get my first dog that was all mine,' he says. 'I went to see the puppies at two days old and picked out a boy – the only male in the litter.'

But when the time came for the puppies to go to their new homes, Peter was in for an unwelcome surprise. His neighbour had promised the male puppy to someone else, a colleague of Peter's who had recently lost his dog.

He was sorely disappointed, but it wasn't all bad news. 'The thing was, every time I went to see the litter, this tiny white puppy with a big black spot on her backside would always be the first one to come up to me,' he says.

Peter took the female puppy home instead, and inspired by the 'ink blot' on her rump, named her Inka.

Almost immediately, the pair became inseparable. Peter would bring home 'buckets' of eye fillet steak and chicken breast from the restaurant he worked at, and it wasn't long before Inka grew into the proportions her bull-mastiff and bull terrier lineage prescribed, eventually tipping the scales at a solid 25 kilograms.

'She was a beautiful dog, with a beautiful coat,' he says proudly. 'And she was really kind, a really soft-hearted dog. She was my little soul mate.'

In 2001, a year after he brought Inka home, Peter left Airlie Beach and relocated to Sydney, almost 2000 kilometres south. He lived at Dee Why on the city's Northern Beaches and cooked at a popular Mexican restaurant there. Suddenly, Inka was forced to adjust from being with Peter virtually every moment of the day to spending long stretches of time at home alone.

'I used to ride my bicycle to the restaurant, and because I worked split shifts I'd come home every afternoon to see her,' he says. 'But she didn't have another dog around her, and coming from Airlie Beach she'd had dogs around her all the time. In the city she was by herself.'

Clearly not content with just her own company, and after several months of being denied 24/7 access to the human she cherished, Inka started escaping from her fenced yard. One night, Peter returned from work and she wasn't there. Frantic, he began to search the area for her – only to have her sheepishly saunter in at 1 a.m., like a teenager caught out after curfew. He wondered if it was his scent – or perhaps the aroma of his gourmet cooking – that had led Inka home.

The next time she disappeared, he received a phone call from a school several kilometres away; she had wandered in and started playing with the children. Fortunately, Inka was microchipped and wore a tag with Peter's phone number on it on her collar, so when he got the call at work he was able to dispatch a friend to collect his roving would-be pupil.

They say calamities come in threes, and it wasn't long before itinerant Inka went wandering again. 'The third time, we'd had a big storm. I came home on my break between shifts and she wasn't there,' Peter recalls. 'I was worried, but I felt confident she would turn up.'

When there was no sign of Inka the next morning, Peter started posting 'lost dog' flyers around the suburb. He telephoned local vet hospitals, but no one had seen her. Still he hoped she would find her way home, following her nose the way he believed she had the first time. It didn't occur to him until much later that the downpour the night before would have washed away her scent trail – and his.

Months went by with no leads, no sightings. It was as if two-year-old Inka had simply vanished. In dark moments, Peter considered the possibility that Inka had died, but he consoled himself with the thought that if she had been run over, someone – perhaps a council worker, or a kind passerby – would have retrieved her tag and let him know.

'The not knowing was the worst thing. I almost wanted someone to say, "She's been hit by a car" because at least then I could have closed the book,' he admits.

Most of the time, Peter was able to convince himself that Inka had been adopted by another family that adored her just as much as he always had. 'I always thought she'd be in a good spot. I told myself that she'd wandered into an old lady's backyard and she's befriended Inka and they've lived happily ever after,' he says.

It was a scenario he clung to when he left Sydney a year later. He was devastated to be leaving without his beloved dog. All he could do was hope she was happy.

Peter bounced around the country, never able to settle, never willing or able to forget his missing dog. Every new place he went, he kept a framed photograph of Inka beside his bed.

Eventually he made Queensland's Gold Coast his home and had a girlfriend who lived just over an hour away at Lennox Head, in the Northern Rivers region of New South Wales. It was not far from there that he met his next canine companion.

Chai had been tied to a fence post at Lismore, 40 kilometres west of Lennox Head, and abandoned by his previous owners. A local rescue group had taken him in, and brought him along to their adopt-a-pet appeal the same day.

'I'd broken up with my girlfriend literally the day before and she had taken our chocolate labrador, so I went along to Lismore to this dog adoption day and Chai put his paw through the cage and kind of grabbed me,' Peter says. 'I said, "What's the story with this one?" and the lady said he was tied to a fence and his owners took off. He was lucky – he was only in the pound for four or five hours before I adopted him.'

Chai settled into life on the Gold Coast with Peter, where he met Janneke in late 2009. They were introduced by mutual friends just before Christmas.

'We met after a Christmas party – my colleagues and I went out dancing, and Peter was one of my colleague's best friends,' says Janneke, who works in training and assessment. 'Part of the reason we got along so well was that I had Barney, and he had Chai.'

During their first date on that Gold Coast beach with their respective four-legged friends in tow, Peter told Janneke the sad story of Inka.

'When he told me about her he was quite emotional. I think he was really gutted about the whole thing. It was like he could never let it go,' she says. 'He was haunted by the fact that maybe he could have done things differently. It was under his skin.'

As they fell in love and Peter shared more stories about his lost dog, Janneke grew to feel like she knew Inka. And like Peter, she hoped for the best. 'We both liked to entertain the thought that some nice family had found her. We hoped, but we just didn't have a clue what had happened to Inka. We never, ever expected that we'd see her again.'

Peter and Janneke married in 2010 – with Chai and Barney in the wedding party, sporting tuxedos – and the following year bought a home on acreage in the Gold Coast suburb of Worongary. They had only been there for a week when, two days before Christmas in 2011 – ten years after Inka vanished – Peter's mobile phone rang.

'I was in the office overlooking our front yard and I got this call from a ranger at Byron Bay Council saying, "We've got your dog here,"' he says. 'I looked outside and I could see Barney and Chai. I said, "No, both of my dogs are here."'

But the caller, Byron Bay ranger Mal Hamilton, was adamant. 'If you're Peter Pignolet,' he told Peter, 'then this is your dog. Her name is Inka.'

Margaret Brown had heard about the dog. As the founder of the Companion Animals Welfare Inc. (CAWI) rescue group, she was the person people called whenever they spotted a sick or stray animal in Brunswick Heads, twenty minutes north of Byron Bay. She had been told about this one a couple of days earlier, when she popped into the Massey Greene caravan park on the banks of the Brunswick River to have dinner with her partner, who lives there.

'I call in there every night to have tea, and some of my partner's neighbours told me there was a very thin dog wandering around the caravan park,' Margaret says. 'There are no cats or dogs permitted in the park, so I said, "Why doesn't somebody catch it and we'll see what we can do for it?"'

Before anyone could secure the dog, however, a man arrived. He was camping across the river, he said, and the dog belonged to him. 'He was a bit of an oddball. He had three other dogs in cages on the tray of his ute, and a cockatoo on the front seat. He was telling people at the park that this dog had cancer, and that was why she was so thin,' she says.

The man took the dog back to his camp, but a couple of days later the scrawny canine appeared in the caravan park again. Concerned for her welfare, residents and holiday-makers tossed her food scraps. It was just a couple of days before Christmas, and the park was full of summer travellers. One kind woman, risking expulsion if she was found with a dog, took the waif in for the night and fed her a more substantial meal.

'People were giving her pies and all sorts of things because they thought she was starving,' says Margaret. 'She must have thought, *I'll head back to that place, those people are giving me pats and food.*'

So Margaret was well aware of Massey Greene's clandestine canine resident, but it was still a surprise to see the dog wander into the CAWI op shop on the Old Pacific Highway, Brunswick Heads' main street. The poor creature was indeed rail thin and absolutely filthy; she looked like she wasn't long for this world.

'The lady who'd kept the dog overnight was very concerned about her, and brought her into the shop,' says Margaret. 'She was very anxious about what was going to happen to her.'

Margaret ran to fetch her microchip scanner. CAWI doesn't have a bricks-and-mortar animal shelter, but operates via a network of foster carers, so the ability to scan an animal wherever it is found is essential. She waved the scanner over the dog and heard a reassuring *BEEP* as a microchip number flashed up. It was good news: somewhere, this dog had an owner, and Margaret doubted it was the man who claimed the dog was his.

Her next call was to Byron Shire Council, where she relayed the chip number to ranger Mal Hamilton. 'He drove up from Byron Bay and got her, then went into the Companion Animals Register – which only the council can do – and we found out she was registered to an address in Sydney.'

The address was Peter Pignolet's former Sydney home, but of course he hadn't lived there for more than a decade and hadn't updated the register with his new details.

But while much had changed in Peter's life in ten years, one thing hadn't.

His phone number.

Peter had to ask Mal to repeat himself. Surely he was hearing things. Was he really saying he had Inka? *His* Inka, with her ink blot bum and her taste for fillet steak? Was Mal truly telling him that Inka had been found ten years and 800 kilometres from where she'd last been seen?

'I said, "Wait, no – I lost her ten years ago!"' Peter says. 'He said he was going to email me some pictures to confirm it was her, because they'd been told she had cancer and she was in a terrible state.'

When the pictures arrived in his inbox, Peter could see immediately that it was indeed his beloved girl, but her emaciated appearance was devastating. Janneke says her husband was stunned by the turn of events.

'Peter just couldn't get his head around it,' she says. 'He was in shock and he had tears in his eyes. I said, "What's going on?" and he said, "They've got Inka!" He was really emotional because she was in such a poor state.'

He was so astonished by the news that Inka was alive, he was at a loss as to what to do next. Mal Hamilton was equally surprised – he'd been expecting to have to arrange to somehow transport Inka to Sydney over the chaotic Christmas travel period, only to discover that Peter now lived just a 45-minute drive from Byron Bay.

'Peter said, "What do I do?" and I said, "You know what you've got to do – you've got to get in the bloody car and drive down there and bring her home!" I had to take a bit of control, because he was completely overwhelmed,' says Janneke. 'My first instinct was to get her home. They'd said she was close to death, and I thought that if that was the case then we had to make sure we were with her for whatever time she had left.'

So Peter did just that. While Janneke attended a Christmas party, he drove south to Byron Bay to collect his long-lost companion. As he drove, he pondered the incredible odds of their reunion. Most people change their mobile phone numbers at least once for one reason or another, but Peter never had. All the other information contained in Inka's microchip registration was out of date. She was less than 100 kilometres away from her rightful home, but if not for those ten digits, he never would have found her.

He thought about where Inka had been all this time, where her journey had taken her and who she had been with. Mal hadn't told him much on the phone. But mostly, Peter wondered if it was possible she might still recognise him after all these years apart.

When they were finally reunited, he was sure she knew him. 'When I got her back she was just as sprightly as she ever was. We drove home from Byron with Inka just sitting there on the passenger seat as if nothing had ever happened,' he says.

Her shocking appearance, however, was heartbreaking proof something *had* happened. As well as being frighteningly underweight, most of Inka's teeth were rotten, she had numerous burn scars on her body and her toenails were so long they had curled over and begun growing painfully into the pads of her paws. 'She'd never been to a vet in her life,' Peter says.

Once he got her home and did take her to the vet, he learned Inka did not have cancer after all. Her deathly appearance was caused by sheer neglect.

The man at the caravan park who had claimed Inka belonged to him was described to Peter as a drifter. He reportedly told police he had been given the dog free of charge by Warringah Council, on Sydney's Northern Beaches. However, the council pound only releases animals to registered owners with proof of identity, and even then they are required to pay pound fees. Peter suspects the man either saw Inka running scared after the storm and picked her up, or stole her right out of his backyard.

'I was told he was a pig hunter, and I think he took her because she was a lovely, solid girl and he thought he could use her to breed – but she was desexed. Dogs were disappearing from around that area at the time. He knew what he was doing,' he says.

The man was never charged with any offence, and he was allowed to keep the other three dogs in his possession, despite determined efforts by CAWI's Margaret Brown and local RSPCA inspectors.

'I felt such guilt when I saw what he had done to her. She had probably been all around Australia on the back of that ute, and she probably would have died there if not for the people at the caravan park,' says Peter. 'I'm just so grateful that I could have her back in my life. The other three dogs may not have been so fortunate.'

Inka's homecoming was both wonderful and surreal. For starters, she 'returned' to a house that was entirely unfamiliar and finding that she had canine siblings she had never seen before – not to mention a new 'mum' in the form of Janneke.

'I've always been an animal lover, and when I saw Inka that first night I was a mess. My heart just went out to her and I knew we had to do everything we could,' she says.

For the first few days, Peter took time off work and slept on the lounge room floor with Inka, waking every half hour to feed her tiny portions of Di-Vetelact, a powdered milk formula usually given to orphaned or early weaned animals. She weighed just 16 kilograms and was so severely mal-nourished it was all her shrunken stomach could cope with (although it wasn't too long before she could manage the eye fillet Peter procured from the restaurant).

'It was a real labour of love, and there wasn't one moment that we didn't fully embrace it,' Janneke recalls. 'We just did what we had to do.'

The change in Inka a month later was remarkable. And after three months, she was virtually unrecognisable as the wraith that had come home from Byron Bay. She'd had her rotten teeth extracted, which meant she could chew on bones with gusto. Her coat shone with health as her weight crept back to 25 kilograms, and she had rediscovered her joie de vivre.

Peter took her back to visit Mal Hamilton and his colleagues at Byron Shire Council. 'I took her back to say thank you and to show them how much she had changed,' he says. 'They couldn't believe it. They said, "This is not Inka!"'

The local newspaper heard about Inka's incredible journey and put her on the front page. Television news reports followed. Under state legislation, Queenslanders require special permission to own more than two dogs, but the local council took Inka's extraordinary circumstances into account and registered her for free.

'When Inka came home, her eyes had this sort of grey film over them. It was like when dogs have cataracts,' says Janneke. 'The vet said it was a sign she was emotionally and physically shutting down. Inka just could not cope with life. To see that disappear, and the light come back into her eyes, was amazing.'

Inka's psychological scars took longer to heal. Once a keen swimmer, she was now strangely hesitant about the water, refusing to venture in deeper than her chest. She would also flinch if anyone tried to pat her head.

Slowly, and after a few false starts, Inka did make friends with her canine counterparts, Chai and Barney. Chai was initially intolerant of Inka and, fearing he was jealous of the new arrival, Peter and Janneke sought the advice of a behaviour specialist. She explained that dogs are highly sensitive to the health of their fellow pack members; it's a throwback to their days as primitive hunters, when their survival depended on every dog pulling his or her weight. Chai was simply registering his objection to having to put up with what he perceived to be a freeloader.

'Chai could sense how sick Inka was and he was basically saying, "This is the most ridiculous decision you've ever made. Why have you brought in this dog that contributes nothing?"' says Janneke. 'Barney was a lot more accepting, and as time went by Inka learned to put Chai in his place if he was having a go at her. It was actually really nice to see, because it meant she was feeling more confident.'

Nevertheless, Janneke and Peter tried to be egalitarian in the distribution of their attention. 'Peter was just so over the moon to have Inka back, so we had to be careful that we shared the love around. There was a lot of negotiation with our furry family!'

Sadly, little more than a year after Peter and Inka were reunited, she did develop cancer. She was about twelve years old. Janneke was now pregnant with the couple's first child, and Peter was desperate for Inka to live to see the baby.

'We went to the vet and he said, "I can't tell you how long. It could be two days, it could be a few weeks." It was actually a few months,' says Peter.

In April 2013, Inka's health suddenly deteriorated. For two days, the Pignolets wrestled with the question of what

to do for their special girl, who had made a truly epic journey in every sense of the word.

'It was heartbreaking. I knew she was old, but seeing
Inka in so much pain was just devastating,' says Peter. 'It
was the worst two days of my life.'

Finally, on 19 April, the couple made the decision to
have Inka put to sleep. Her journey was finally at an end.

Three months later, on 20 July, their son, Charlie, was
born. Though he was never able to meet Inka, he has heard
her incredible tale many times, and knows that the big frangi-
pani tree in the garden is her resting place.

Peter still gets emotional when he talks about brave,
determined Inka. He's grateful he had the chance to make her
final months as comfortable and love-filled as she deserved.
As Janneke says, 'Sometimes you give up, but there is always
hope in the world.'

Peter is adamant that Inka's microchip was the reason
they were able to find each other again. Maybe it was.
Maybe it was something else.

Maybe it was love.

MORE INFORMATION

OCCY

RSPCA New South Wales
rspcansw.org.au

LUDIVINE

facebook.com/runludivinerun

Elkmont's Hound Dog Half Marathon
runsignup.com/Race/AL/Elkmont/ElkmontHalfMarathon
facebook.com/Elkmonts-Hound-Dog-Half-1647029648910689/

OSCAR

Oscar's Arc
oscarsarc.org

World Woof Tour
worldwooftour.com

BONNIE

RSPCA Victoria
rspcavic.org

Salvation Army
salvos.org.au

ILY

Sherry Petta Rescue
sherrypetta-rescue.com
facebook.com/SherryPettaRescue

RAMA

Animals SOS Sri Lanka
animalsos-sl.com
facebook.com/Animal-SOS-Sri-Lanka-165576613502654/

CHOPPER

Lort Smith Animal Hospital
lortsmith.com

TILLIE AND PHOEBE

Vashon Island Pet Protectors
vipp.org

IDITAROD

Iditarod Trail Sled Dog Race
iditarod.com

INKA

Companion Animals Welfare Inc (CAWI)
cawi.org.au

ACKNOWLEDGEMENTS

I am enormously grateful to all the wonderful dog owners who shared their pets' incredible tales with me. Meeting you all – even when it was only via phone or Skype – has been a great privilege, and I really can't thank you enough for trusting me with your stories. The bond you all share with your pets is deep and profound, and in these pages I've tried my very best to capture that and convey what truly special animals they are.

I'm also indebted to a great number of brilliant behind-the-scenes people who assisted in putting me in touch with some harder-to-find dog owners, and helped out with background research and images. So endless thanks and plaudits to:

Occy: Philippa and Nathan Johnston; Binny Murray; Jessica Conway at RSPCA NSW.

Ludivine: April Hamlin; Gretta Armstrong.

Oscar: Joanne Lefson; Belinda Abraham at Cape of Good Hope SPCA, South Africa.

Bonnie: John Laffan; Sharon Mackenzie at RSPCA Victoria; Mitch Ryan and Captain Bronwyn Williams at The Salvation Army.

Sissy: Nancy Franck; Sarah Wood; Samantha Conrad and Karen Vander Sanden at Mercy Medical Center, Cedar Rapids, Iowa.

Carry: David and Jen Winfield.

Rosie: Alice Bennett and family; Debra Tranter at Oscar's Law.

Ily: Rose Sharman; Sherry Petta; Linda Weitzman.

Rama: Kim and Gary Cooling.

Chopper/Fergus: Romy Panzera; Serena Horg and Caroline Ottinger at Lort Smith Animal Hospital, Melbourne; Jane Evans.

Penny: Kendra and Colt Brown.

Jay: Chris Jones; Craig Treloar at City of Salisbury.

Tillie and Phoebe: BJ Duft; Tom Conway at Tall Clover Farm.

Pero: Shan and Alan James.

Lucky and Bella: Michele Martin.

Dinah: Jamila El Maroudi.

Iditarod: Christian Turner.

Inka: Peter and Janneke Pignolet; Margaret Brown at Companion Animals Welfare Inc (CAWI), Brunswick Heads; Donna Johnston at Byron Shire Council.

Thanks also to my own dogs' wonderful vet, Kay Gerry from Sydney Road Veterinary Clinic, for answering my many doggy research questions!

A million thanks to Sarah Fairhall at Penguin Random House for thinking of me when you needed a 'crazy dog lady' to tackle a book of dog stories, and also for your thoughtful edits on the manuscript. Hats off to copyeditor extraordinaire Andrea Davison for polishing the finished product.

And last but most definitely by no means least, thank you Mark for your unwavering support, endless cups of tea and countless weekends entertaining the toddler while I sat at the dining table and wrote about dogs. You're three-quarters of the reason this book got finished.